T0222590

Lecture Notes in Computer Science   **8921**

Commenced Publication in 1973
Founding and Former Series Editors:
Gerhard Goos, Juris Hartmanis, and Jan van Leeuwen

More information about this series at http://www.springer.com/series/7409

Arun Jagatheesan · Justin Levandoski
Thomas Neumann · Andrew Pavlo (Eds.)

In Memory Data Management and Analysis

First and Second International Workshops
IMDM 2013, Riva del Garda, Italy,
August 26, 2013
IMDM 2014, Hongzhou, China,
September 1, 2014
Revised Selected Papers

 Springer

Editors
Arun Jagatheesan
Samsung Corporation
San Jose, CA
USA

Justin Levandoski
Microsoft Corporation
Redmond, WA
USA

Thomas Neumann
Technische Universität München
Garching
Germany

Andrew Pavlo
Computer Science Department
Carnegie Mellon University
Pittsburgh, PA
USA

ISSN 0302-9743   ISSN 1611-3349   (electronic)
Lecture Notes in Computer Science
ISBN 978-3-319-13959-3   ISBN 978-3-319-13960-9   (eBook)
DOI 10.1007/978-3-319-13960-9

Library of Congress Control Number: 2014960149

LNCS Sublibrary: SL3 – Information Systems and Applications, incl. Internet/Web, and HCI

Springer Cham Heidelberg New York Dordrecht London

Printed on acid-free paper

Springer International Publishing AG Switzerland is part of Springer Science+Business Media
(www.springer.com)

Preface

Over the last 30 years, memory prices have been dropping by a factor of 10 every 5 years. The number of I/O operations per second (IOPS) in DRAM is far greater than other storage media such as hard disks and SSDs. DRAM is readily available in the market at better price point in comparison to DRAM-alternatives. These trends make DRAM a better storage media for latency-sensitive data management applications. For example, mobile applications require low-latency responses to user requests. The "hot set" of large transactional workloads fit comfortably in memory. Many large-scale web applications such as Facebook and Amazon manage most of their active data in main memory. With the emergence of such a diverse pool of latency-sensitive applications coupled with dropping DRAM prices, it is timely to explore main-memory optimized data management platforms.

In addition, almost all major database vendors offer (or plan to offer) main-memory optimized database solutions. Examples include solidDB from IBM, Hekaton from Microsoft, TimesTen and Exalytics from Oracle, HANA from SAP, and startups such as MemSQL and VoltDB. Such interest from most major vendors clearly shows the emerging trend and the need for further research in this direction.

We organized the In-Memory Data Management and Analytics workshop (IMDM) to bring together researchers and practitioners interested in the proliferation of in-memory data management and analytics infrastructures. The workshop is a forum to present research challenges, novel ideas, and methodologies that can improve in-memory (main memory) data management and analytics. These proceedings contain papers from both the 2013 and 2014 workshops colocated with VLDB in Trento, Italy and Hangzhou, China, respectively. Both workshops were well attended and sparked interesting technical discussions spanning themes from main-memory graph analytics platforms to main-memory OLTP applications.

All papers in these proceedings were peer reviewed by an expert Program Committee comprised of experts from both industry and academia. We would like to thank these committee members as well as the authors for contributing high-quality work.

September 2014

Arun Jagatheesan
Justin Levandoski
Thomas Neumann
Andrew Pavlo

Organization

Workshop Organizers

Arun Jagatheesan   Samsung R&D Center, USA
Justin Levandoski   Microsoft Research, USA
Thomas Neumann   Technische Universität München, Germany
Andrew Pavlo   Carnegie Mellon University, USA

Program Committee for IMDM 2013

Shel Finkelstein   SAP Labs, USA
Yongqiang He   Facebook, USA
Jens Krüger   Hasso Plattner Institute, Germany
Per-Åke Larson   Microsoft Research, USA
Wolfgang Lehner   TU Dresden, Germany
Stefan Manegold   Centrum Wiskunde & Informatica,
    The Netherlands
Ippokratis Pandis   IBM Research, USA
Jignesh Patel   University of Wisconsin–Madison, USA
Shankar Raman   IBM Research, USA
Sandeep Tata   Google, USA

Program Committee for IMDM 2014

Spyros Blanas   Ohio State University, USA
Shel Finkelstein   Independent
Ryan Johnson   University of Toronto, Canada
Hideaki Kimura   HP Labs, USA
Jens Krüger   Hasso Plattner Institute, Germany
Wolfgang Lehner   TU Dresden, Germany
Stefan Manegold   Centrum Wiskunde & Informatica,
    The Netherlands
Ippokratis Pandis   Cloudera, USA
Ryan Stutsman   Microsoft Research, USA
Sandeep Tata   Google, USA
Pinar Tozun   École Polytechnique Fédérale de Lausanne,
    Switzerland

Contents

IMDM 2013 Workshop Papers

Massively Parallel NUMA-Aware Hash Joins

Harald Lang, Viktor Leis$^{(\boxtimes)}$, Martina-Cezara Albutiu,
Thomas Neumann, and Alfons Kemper

Technische Universität München, Munich, Germany
{harald.lang,viktor.leis,martina-cezara.albutiu,
thomas.neumann,alfons.kemper}@in.tum.de

Abstract. Driven by the two main hardware trends increasing main
memory and massively parallel multi-core processing in the past few
years, there has been much research effort in parallelizing well-known
join algorithms. However, the non-uniform memory access (NUMA) of
these architectures to main memory has only gained limited attention
in the design of these algorithms. We study recent proposals of main
memory hash join implementations and identify their major performance
problems on NUMA architectures. We then develop a NUMA-aware
hash join for massively parallel environments, and show how the specific implementation details affect the performance on a NUMA system.
Our experimental evaluation shows that a carefully engineered hash join
implementation outperforms previous high performance hash joins by a
factor of more than two, resulting in an unprecedented throughput of
3/4 billion join argument quintuples per second.

1 Introduction

The recent developments of hardware providing huge main memory capacities
and a large number of cores led to the emergence of main memory database
systems and a high research effort in the context of parallel database operators.
In particular, the probably most important operator, the equi-join, has been
investigated. Blanas et al. [1] and Kim et al. [2] presented very high performing
implementations of hash join operators.

So far, those algorithms only considered hardware environments with uniform
access latency and bandwidth over the complete main memory. With the advent
of architectures which scale main memory via non-uniform memory access, the
need for NUMA-aware algorithms arises. While in [3] we redesigned the classic
sort/merge join for multi-core NUMA machines, we now concentrate on redesigning the other classic join method, the hash join.

In this paper we present our approach of a NUMA-aware hash join. We optimized parallel hash table construction via a lock-free synchronization mechanism
based on optimistic validation instead of a costly pessimistic locking/latching, as
illustrated in Fig. 1. Also, we devised a NUMA-optimized storage layout for the
hash table in order to effectively utilize the aggregated memory bandwidth of all
NUMA nodes. In addition, we engineered the hash table such that (unavoidable)

© Springer International Publishing Switzerland 2015
A. Jagatheesan et al. (Eds.): IMDM 2013/2014, LNCS 8921, pp. 3–14, 2015.
DOI: 10.1007/978-3-319-13960-9_1

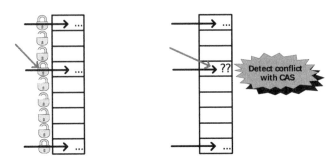

Fig. 1. Pessimistic vs. optimistic write access to a hash table

collisions are locally consolidated, i.e., within the same cache line. These improvements resulted in a performance gain of an order of magnitude compared to the recently published multi-core hash join of Blanas et al. [1]. Meanwhile Balkesen et al. [4] also studied the results of [1] and published hardware optimized re-implementations of those algorithms [5] which also far outperform the previous ones. Although, they focused their research on multi-core CPU architectures with uniform memory access, their source code contains rudimentary NUMA support which improves performance by a factor of 4 on our NUMA machine.

Throughout the paper we refer to the hash join algorithms as described in [1]:

1. **No** partitioning join: A simple algorithm without a partitioning phase that creates a single shared hash table during the build phase.
2. **Shared** partitioning join: Both input relations are partitioned. Thereby, the target partitions' write buffers are shared among all threads.
3. **Independent** partitioning join: All threads perform the partitioning phase independently from each other. They first locally create parts of the target partitions which are linked together after all threads have finished their (independent) work.
4. **Radix** partitioning join: Both input relations are radix-partitioned in parallel. The partitioning is done in multiple passes by applying the algorithm recursively. The algorithm was originally proposed by Manegold et al. [6] and further revised in [2].

We started to work with the original code provided by Blanas et al. on a system with uniform memory access, on which we were able to reproduce the published results. By contrast, when executing the code on our NUMA system (which is described in Sect. 4) we noticed a decreased performance with all algorithms. We identified three major problems of the algorithms.

1. **Fine-grained locking** while building the hash table reduces parallelism, which is not just NUMA related, but becomes more critical with an increasing number of concurrently running threads.

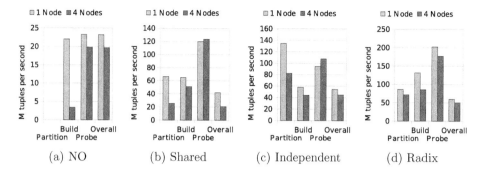

Fig. 2. Performance of the algorithms presented in [1] on a NUMA system, when 8 threads are restricted to 1 memory node, or distributed over 4 nodes

2. **Extensive remote memory accesses** to shared data structures (e.g., the shared partitions' write buffers of the radix partitioning join) which reside within a single NUMA node. This results in link contention and thus decreased performance.
3. **Accessing multiple memory locations within a tight loop** increases latencies and creates additional overhead by the cache coherence protocol which is more costly on NUMA systems.

In the following section we examine the effects on the given implementations that are mostly caused by non-uniform memory accesses. In Sect. 3 we focus on how to implement a hash join operator in a NUMA-aware way. Here we address the main challenges for hash join algorithms on modern architectures: Reduce synchronization costs, reduce random access patterns to memory, and optimize for limited memory bandwidth. The results of the experimental evaluations are discussed in Sect. 4.

2 NUMA Effects

To make the NUMA effects visible (and the changes comparable) we re-ran the original experiments with the *uniform data set* in two different configurations. First we employed eight threads on eight physical cores within a single NUMA node, thereby simulating a uniform-memory-access machine. Then, we distributed the threads equally over all 4 nodes, i.e., 2 cores per node.

Figure 2 shows the performance[1] of the individual hash join implementations. It gives an overview how the join phases are influenced by NUMA effects. The performance of all implementations decreases. Only the shared-partitioning and the independent-partitioning algorithms show a slightly better performance during the probe phase. The no-partitioning and shared-partitioning algorithms are

---

[1] Throughout the paper we refer to M as 2^{20} and to the *overall performance* as $(|R| + |S|)/runtime$.

most affected at the build and the partition phase, respectively. In both phases they extensively write to shared data structures. The build performance drops by 85 % and the performance of the partitioning phase by 62 %. The overall performance decreases by 25 % in average in the given scenario.

In contrast to the original results we can see that the build performance is always slower than the probe performance, which we provoked by shuffling the input. However, due to synchronization overhead it is reasonable that building a hash table is slower than probing it. Therefore, the build phase becomes more important, especially when the ratio $|R|/|S|$ becomes greater. This is why in the following section we pay special attention to the build phase.

3   NUMA-Aware Hash Join

3.1   Synchronization

Synchronization in a hash join with a single shared hash table is intensively needed during the build phase where the build input is read and the tuples are copied to their corresponding hash buckets. Here it is guaranteed that the hash table will not be probed until the build phase has been finished. Additionally, it will no longer be modified after the build phase has been finished. Therefore no synchronization is necessary during the later probe phase. Another crucial part are the write buffers which are accessed concurrently. Especially the shared partitioning algorithm makes heavy use of locks during the partitioning phase where all threads write concurrently to the same buffers. This causes higher lock contention with an increasing number of threads. In this paper we only focus on the synchronization aspects of hash tables.

There are many ways to implement a thread safe hash table. One fundamental design decision is the synchronization mechanism. The implementation provided by Blanas et al. [1] uses a very concise *spin-lock* which only reserves a single byte in memory. Each lock protects a single hash bucket, whereas each bucket can store two tuples. In the given implementation, all locks are stored within an additional contiguous array. Unfortunately, this design decision has some drawbacks that affect the build phase. For every write access to the hash table, we have to access (at least) two different cache lines. The one that holds the lock is accessed twice: Once for acquiring and once for releasing the lock after the bucket has been modified. This greatly increases memory latencies and has been identified as one of the three major bottlenecks (listed in Sect. 1). We can reduce the negative effects by modifying the buckets' data structure so that each bucket additionally holds its corresponding lock. Balkesen et al. [4] also identified this as a bottleneck on systems with uniform memory access. Especially on NUMA systems, we have to deal with higher latencies and we therefore expect an even higher impact on the build performance. In the later experimental evaluation (Sect. 4) we show how lock placement affects the performance of our own hash table. We also consider the case where a single lock is responsible for multiple hash buckets.

For our hash table we use an optimistic, lock-free approach instead of locks. The design was motivated by the observation that hash tables for a join are insert-only during the build phase, then lookup-only during the probe phase, but updates and deletions are not performed. The buckets are implemented as triples (h, k, v), where h contains the hash value of the key k and v holds the value (payload). In all our experiments we (realistically for large databases) use 8 bytes of memory for each component. We use h as a marker which signals whether a bucket is empty or already in use. During the build phase, the threads first check if the marker is set. If the corresponding bucket is empty they exchange the value zero by the hash value within an atomic *Compare-and-Swap* operation (CAS). If meanwhile the marker has already been set by another thread, the atomic operation fails and we linearly probe, i.e., try again on the next write position. Once the CAS operation succeeds the corresponding thread implicitly has exclusive write access to the corresponding bucket and no further synchronization is needed for storing the tuple. We only have to establish a barrier between the two phases to ensure that all key-value pairs have been written before we start probing the hash table.

3.2   Memory Allocation

In this section we describe the effects of local and remote memory access as well as what programmers have to consider when allocating and initializing main memory. On NUMA systems we can directly access all available memory. However, accessing local memory is cheaper than accessing remote memory. The costs depend on how the NUMA partitions are connected and therefore this is hardware dependent. In our system the four nodes are fully connected though we always need to pass exactly one QPI link (hop) when accessing remote memory. By default the system allocates memory within the memory node that the requesting thread is running on. This behavior can be changed by using the numactl tool. In particular, the command line argument -interleave=all tells the operating system to interleave memory allocations among all available nodes, an option which non-NUMA aware programs may benefit from. It might be an indicator for optimization potential if a program runs faster on interleaved memory, whereas NUMA-aware programs may suffer due to loss of control over memory allocations. We show these effects in our experiments.

For data intensive algorithms we have to consider where to place the data the algorithm operates on. In C++ memory is usually allocated dynamically using the *new* operator or the *malloc* function. This simply reserves memory but as long as the newly allocated memory has not been initialized (e.g., by using *memset*) the memory is not pinned to a specific NUMA-node. The first access places the destination page within a specific node. If the size of the requested memory exceeds the page size, the memory will then only be partially pinned and does not affect the remaining untouched space. A single contiguous memory area can therefore be distributed among all nodes as long as the number of nodes is less than or equal to the number of memory pages. This can be exposed to keep the implementations simple by just loosing a reasonable amount of control and granularity with respect to data placement.

For evaluation we started with a naive implementation which we improved step-by-step. Our goal was to develop a hash join implementation that performs best when using non-interleaved memory because running a whole DBMS process in interleaved mode might not be an option in real world scenarios. We also avoided to add additional parameters to the hash join, and we do not want to constrain our implementation to a particular hardware layout. We consider the general case that the input is equally distributed across the nodes and the corresponding memory location is known to the "nearest" worker thread. We will show that interleaved memory increases performance of non-NUMA-aware implementations, but we will also show in the following section that our hash join performs even better when we take care about the memory allocations by ourselves than leaving it to the operating system.

3.3 Hash Table Design

Hash tables basically use one of two strategies for collision handling: *chaining* or *open addressing*. With chaining, the hash table itself contains only pointers, buckets are allocated on demand and linked to the hash table (or previous buckets). With open addressing, collisions are handled within the hash table itself. That is, when the bucket that a key hashes to is full, more buckets are checked according to a certain *probe sequence* (e.g., linear probing, quadratic probing, etc.). For open addressing we focus on linear probing as this provides higher cache locality than other probe sequences, because a collision during insert as well as during probing likely hits the same cache line. Both strategies have their strengths. While chaining provides better performance during the build phase, linear probing has higher throughput during the probe phase. For real world scenarios the build input is typically (much) smaller than the probe input. We therefore chose to employ linear probing for our hash join implementation.

It is well known that the performance of open addressing degenerates if the hash table becomes too full. In practice, this can be a problem because the exact input size is generally not known, and query optimization estimates can be wrong by orders of magnitude. Therefore, we propose to materialize the build input before starting the build phase, then the hash table can be constructed with the correct size. Since the materialization consists of sequential writes whereas hash table construction has a random access pattern, this only about 10 % overhead to the build phase. Note that our experiments do not include this materialization phase.

3.4 Implementation Details

In Listing 1.1 we sketch the insert function of our hash table. In line 2 we compute the hash value of the given key (more details on hash functions in Sect. 4.3) and in line 3 the bucket number is computed by masking all bits of the hash value to zero that would exceed the hash table's size. The size of the hash table is always a power of two and the number of buckets is set to at least twice the size of the build input. Thus, for n input tuples we get the number of buckets $b = 2^{\lceil log_2(n) \rceil + 1}$ and the $mask = b - 1$. The relatively generous space consumption for the hash table is more than compensated by the fact that the probe input, which is often orders of magnitude larger than the build input, can be kept in-place. The radix join, in contrast, partitions both input relations.

Listing 1.1. Insert function

```
1   insertAtomic(uint64_t key, uint64_t value) {
2     uint64_t hash = hashFunction(key);
3     uint64_t pos = hash & mask;
4     while (table[pos].h != 0 || (! CAS(&table[pos].h, 0, hash))) {
5       pos = (pos + 1) & mask;
6     }
7     table[pos].k = key;
8     table[pos].v = value;
9   }
```

Within the condition of the while loop (line 4) we first check, if the bucket is empty. If this is the case the atomic CAS function is called as described in Sect. 3.1. If either the hash value does not equal zero[2] or the CAS function returns `false`, the bucket number (write position) is incremented and we try again. Once the control flow reaches line 7 the current thread has gained write access to the bucket at position `pos` where the key-value pair is stored.

The notable aspect here is that there is no corresponding operation for releasing an acquired lock. Usually a thread acquires a lock, modifies the bucket, and finally gives up the lock, which establishes a happened-before relationship between modification and unlocking. In our implementation the CPU is free to defer the modification or to execute them in an out of order manner because we do not have any data dependencies until the probe phase starts. Further, we optimized for sequential memory accesses in case of collisions by applying the open addressing scheme with a linear probing sequence for collision resolution. This strategy leads to a well predictable access pattern which the hardware prefetcher can exploit.

4   Evaluation

We conducted our experiments on a Linux server (kernel 3.5.0) with 1 TB main memory and 4 Intel Xeon X7560 CPUs clocked at 2.27 GHz with 8 physical cores (16 hardware contexts) each, resulting in a total of 32 cores and, due to hyperthreading, 64 hardware contexts. Unless stated otherwise we use all available hardware contexts.

---

[2] *hashFunction* sets the most significant bit of the hash value to 1 and thus ensures no hash value equals 0. This limits the hash domain to 2^{63}, but does not increase the number of collisions, since the least significant bits determine the hash table position.

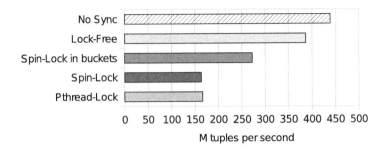

Fig. 3. Build performance using different synchronization mechanisms

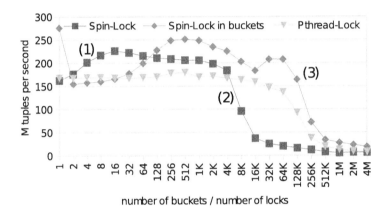

Fig. 4. Effects of lock-striping on the build phase

4.1 Synchronization

In our first experiment we measure the effect of different synchronization mechanisms on build performance. To reduce measurement variations we increased the cardinality of the build input R to 128 M tuples. Again we used a uniform data set with unique 64 bit join keys. The results are shown in Fig. 3. We compared the original spin-lock implementation with the POSIX-threads mutex and our lock-free implementation. While the spin-lock and the pthreads implementation offer almost the same performance, our lock-free implementation outperforms them by factor 2.3. We can also see a performance improvement of 1.7 x when placing the lock within the hash bucket instead of placing all locks in a separate (contiguous) memory area. The hatched bar (labeled "No Sync") represents the theoretical value for the case where synchronization costs would be zero.

In the second experiment we reduce the number of locks that are synchronizing write accesses to the hash buckets. We start with one lock per bucket and successively halve the number of locks in every run. Therefore a lock becomes responsible for multiple hash buckets ("lock striping"). The right-hand side of Fig. 4 shows that too few locks result in bad performance because of too many lock conflicts. The best performance is achieved when the number of locks is such that all locks fit into cache, but collisions are unlikely.

The experiments confirmed that an efficient lock implementation is crucial for the build phase. It also showed that protecting multiple buckets with a single lock indeed can have positive effects on the performance but cannot compete with a lock-free implementation. Especially the first two data points of the "Spin-Lock in buckets" curve show that on NUMA architectures writing to two different cache lines within a tight loop can cause crucial performance differences.

4.2 Memory Allocation

For the experimental evaluation of the different memory allocation strategies we consider the build and the probe phase separately. We focus on how they are affected by those strategies, but we also plot the overall performance for completeness. To get good visual results we set the cardinality of both relations to the same value (128 M). During all experiments we only count and do not materialize the output tuples. We use the following four setups:

(1) **non-NUMA-aware:** The input data and the hash table are stored on a single NUMA node.
(2) **interleaved:** All memory pages are interleaved round-robin between the NUMA nodes.
(3) **NUMA-aware/dynamic:** The input relations are thread-local whereas the hash tables' memory pages at initialized dynamically during the build phase[3].
(4) **NUMA-aware:** The input data is thread-local and the hash table is (manually) interleaved across all NUMA nodes.

Figure 5 shows the results of all four experiments. We measured the performance of the build and probe phase as well as the overall performance in M tuples per second. The distributed memory allocation of the hash table in (4) is done as follows: We divide the size of the hash table into i equally sized chunks of size 2 MB and let them be initialized by all threads in parallel where the ith chunk is "memsetted" by thread i mod #threads.

We can see an improvement by a factor of more than three just by using interleaved memory, because in the non-NUMA-aware setup the memory bandwidth of one NUMA node is saturated and thus becomes the bottleneck. When comparing setup (3) with (2) a decreased performance during the build phase can be seen which is caused by the dynamic allocation of the hash tables' memory. Finally the 4th setup shows the best performance. Our own implementation, that simulates an interleaved memory only for the hash tables' memory achieves (approximately) the same build performance as in the second setup, but we can increase the performance of the probe phase by additional 188 mtps, because we

---

[3] When a page is first written to, it is assigned to the memory node of the writing thread, which usually results in pseudo-random assignment.

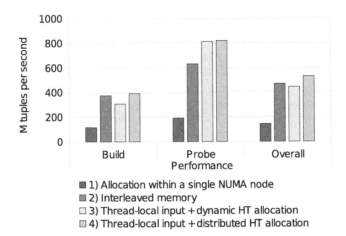

Fig. 5. Experimental results of different data placement/memory allocation strategies

Table 1. Performance comparisons NO vs. Radix (key/foreign-key join)

$|R|/|S|$	our NO	Radix [5]
16 M/16 M	503 mtps	147 mtps
16 M/160 M	742 mtps	346 mtps
32 M/32 M	505 mtps	142 mtps
32 M/320 M	740 mtps	280 mtps
1 G/1 G	493 mtps	-
1 G/10 G	682 mtps	-

can read the probe input from interleaved memory. It is a reasonable assumption that in practice the relations are (equally) distributed across all memory partitions and we only need to assign the nearest input to each thread.

Table 1 shows comparisons with the Radix join implementation of [5]. Unfortunately, this implementation crashed for extremely large workloads such as 1 G/10 G (176 GB of data). For comparison, the TPC-H record holder Vector-Wise achieves 50 mtps for such large joins [3].

4.3   Hash Functions

In accordance to previous publications, and in order to obtain comparable performance results, we used the modulo hash function (implemented using a logical AND, as discussed in Sect. 3.4) in all experiments. In this section we study the influence of hash functions on join performance. On the one hand, modulo hashing is extremely fast and has good join performance in micro benchmarks. On the other hand, it is quite easy to construct workloads that cause dramatic performance degradation. For example, instead of using consecutive integers, we left gaps between the join keys so that only every tenth value of the key space was used. As a consequence, we measured a 84 % decrease performance for the NO implementation of [5]. Whereas our implementation is affected by power-of-two gaps, and slows down by 63 % when we use a join key distance of 16.

We evaluated a small number of hash functions (Murmur64A, CRC, and Fibonacci hashing) with our hash join implementation. It turned out that the Murmur hash always offers (almost) the same performance independent from the tested workload. At the same time it is the most expensive hash function, which reduces the overall join performance by 36 % (over modulo hashing with consecutive keys). The CRC function is available as a hardware instruction on modern CPUs with the SSE 4.2 instruction set and therefore reduces the performance by less than 1 % in most cases. However, it is less robust than Murmur, for some workloads it caused significantly more collisions than Murmur. The Fibonacci hash function, which consists of a multiplication with a magic constant, offered almost the same performance as modulo, but unfortunately had the same weaknesses.

Real-world hashing naturally incurs higher cost, but does not affect all algorithms equally. Employing a costly hash function affects the Radix join more than the NO join, because the hash function is evaluated multiple times for each tuple (during each partitioning phase, and in the final probe phase). Finally, using more realistic hash functions makes the results more comparable to algorithms that do not use hashing like sort/merge joins.

5 Related Work

Parallel join processing has been investigated extensively, in particular since the advent of main memory databases. Thereby, most approaches are based on the radix join, which was pioneered by the MonetDB group [6,7]. This join method improves cache locality by continuously partitioning into ever smaller chunks that ultimately fit into the cache. Ailamaki et al. [8] improved cache locality during the probing phase of the hash join using software controlled prefetching. Our hash join virtually always incurs only one cache miss per lookup or insert, due open addressing.

An Intel/Oracle team [2] adapted hash join to multi-core CPUs. They also investigated sort-merge join and hypothesized that due to architectural trends of wider SIMD, more cores, and smaller memory bandwidth per core sort-merge join is likely to outperform hash join on upcoming chip multiprocessors. Blanas et al. [1,9] and Balkesen et al. [4,5] presented even better performance results for their parallel hash join variants. However, these algorithms are not optimized for NUMA environments.

Albutiu et al. [3] presented a NUMA-aware design of sort-based join algorithms, which was improved by Li et al. [10] to avoid cross-traffic.

6   Summary and Conclusions

Modern hardware architectures with huge main memory capacities and increasing number of cores have led to the development of highly parallel in-memory hash join algorithms [1,2] for main memory database systems. However, prior work did not yet consider architectures with non-uniform memory access. We identified the challenges that NUMA poses to hash join algorithms. Based on our findings we developed our own algorithm which uses optimistic validation instead of costly pessimistic locking. Our algorithm distributes data carefully in order to provide balanced bandwidth on the inter-partition links. At the same time, no architecture-specific knowledge is required, i.e., the algorithm is oblivious to the specific NUMA topology. Our hash join outperforms previous parallel hash join implementations on a NUMA system. We further found that our highly parallel shared hash table implementation performs better than radix partitioned variants because these incur a high overhead for partitioning. This is the case although hash joins inherently do not exhibit cache locality as they are inserting and probing the hash table randomly. But at least we could avoid additional cache misses due to collisions by employing linear probing. We therefore conclude that cache effects are less decisive for multi-core hash joins. On large setups we achieved a join performance of more than 740 M tuples per second, which is more than 2 x compared to the best known radix join published in [5] and one order of magnitude faster than the best-in-breed commercial database system VectorWise.

References

1. Blanas, S., Li, Y., Patel, J.M.: Design and evaluation of main memory hash join algorithms for multi-core CPUs. In: SIGMOD (2011)
2. Kim, C., Sedlar, E., Chhugani, J., Kaldewey, T., Nguyen, A.D., Blas, A.D., Lee, V.W., Satish, N., Dubey, P.: Sort vs. hash revisited: fast join implementation on modern multi-core CPUs. PVLDB **2**, 1378–1389 (2009)
3. Albutiu, M.C., Kemper, A., Neumann, T.: Massively parallel sort-merge joins in main memory multi-core database systems. PVLDB **5**, 1064–1075 (2012)
4. Balkesen, C., Teubner, J., Alonso, G., Özsu, T.: Main-memory hash joins on multi-core CPUs: tuning to the underlying hardware. In: ICDE (2013)
5. Balkesen, C., Teubner, J., Alonso, G., Özsu, T.: Source code. (http://www.systems.ethz.ch/sites/default/files/multicore-hashjoins-0_1_tar.gz)
6. Manegold, S., Boncz, P.A., Kersten, M.L.: Optimizing main-memory join on modern hardware. IEEE Trans. Knowl. Data Eng. **14**, 709–730 (2002)
7. Boncz, P.A., Manegold, S., Kersten, M.L.: Database architecture optimized for the new bottleneck: memory access. In: VLDB (1999)
8. Chen, S., Ailamaki, A., Gibbons, P.B., Mowry, T.C.: Improving hash join performance through prefetching. ACM Trans. Database Syst. **32** (2007)
9. Blanas, S., Patel, J.M.: How efficient is our radix join implementation? (2011). http://pages.cs.wisc.edu/sblanas/files/comparison.pdf
10. Li, Y., Pandis, I., Mueller, R., Raman, V., Lohman, G.: NUMA-aware algorithms: the case of data shuffling. In: CIDR (2013)

Fast Column Scans: Paged Indices for In-Memory Column Stores

Martin Faust[(⊠)], David Schwalb, and Jens Krueger

Hasso Plattner Institute, University of Potsdam,
Prof.-Dr.-Helmert-Str. 2-3, 14482 Potsdam, Germany
{martin.faust,david.schwalb,jens.krueger}@hpi.de

Abstract. Commodity hardware is available in configurations with huge amounts of main memory and it is viable to keep large databases of enterprises in the RAM of one or a few machines. Additionally, a reunification of transactional and analytical systems has been proposed to enable operational reporting on the most recent data. In-memory column stores appeared in academia and industry as a solution to handle the resulting mixed workload of transactional and analytical queries. Therein queries are processed by scanning whole columns to evaluate the predicates on non-key columns. This leads to a waste of memory bandwidth and reduced throughput.

In this work we present the Paged Index, an index tailored towards dictionary-encoded columns. The indexing concept builds upon the availability of the indexed data at high speeds, a situation that is unique to in-memory databases. By reducing the search scope we achieve up to two orders of magnitude of performance increase for the column scan operation during query runtime.

1 Introduction

Enterprise systems often process a read-mostly workload [5] and consequently in-memory columns stores tailored towards this workload hold the majority of table data in a read-optimized partition [9]. To apply predicates, this partition is scanned in its compressed form through the intensive use of the SIMD units of modern CPUs. Although this operation is fast when compared to disk-based systems, its performance can be increased if we decrease the search scope and thereby the amount of data that needs to be streamed from main memory to the CPU. The resulting savings of memory bandwidth lead to a better utilization of this scarce resource, which allows to process more queries with equally sized machines.

2 Background and Prior Work

In this section we briefly summarize our prototypical database system, the used compression technique and refer to prior work.

© Springer International Publishing Switzerland 2015
A. Jagatheesan et al. (Eds.): IMDM 2013/2014, LNCS 8921, pp. 15–27, 2015.
DOI: 10.1007/978-3-319-13960-9_2

2.1   Column Stores with a Read-Optimized Partition

Column stores are in the focus of research [10–12], because their performance characteristics enable superior analytical (OLAP) performance, while keeping the data in-memory still allows a sufficient transactional performance for many usecases. Consequently, Plattner [6] proposed, that in-memory column stores can handle a mixed workload of transactional (OLTP) and analytical queries and become the single source of truth in future enterprise applications.

Dictionary Compressed Column. Our prototypical implementation stores all table data vertically partitioned in dictionary compressed columns. The values are represented by bit-packed value-ids, which reference the actual, uncompressed values within a sorted dictionary by their offset. Dictionary compressed columns can be found in HYRISE [3], SanssouciDB [7] and SAP HANA [9].

Enterprise Data. As shown by Krueger et al. [5], enterprise data consists of many sparse columns. The domain of values is often limited, because there is a limited number of underlying options in the business processes. For example, only a relatively small number of customers, appears in the typically large order table. Additionally, data within some columns often correlates in regard to its position. Consider a column storing the *promised delivery date* in the *orders* table. Although the dates will not be ordered, because different products will have different delivery time spans, the data will follow a general trend. In this work, we want to focus on columns that exhibit such properties.

Related Work. Important work on main-memory indices has been done by Rao and Ross [8], but their indexing method applies to the value-id lookup in sorted dictionaries rather then the position lookup that we will focus on in this paper. Since they focus on Decision Support Systems (DSS), they claim that an index rebuild after every bulk-load is viable. In this paper we assume a mixed-workload system, where the merge-performance must be kept as high as possible, hence we reuse the old index to build an updated index.

Idreos et al. [4] present indices for in-memory column stores that are build during query execution, and adapt to changing workloads, however the integration of the indexing schemes into the frequent merge process of the write-optimized and read-only store is missing.

Graefe [2] evaluates a related indexing techniques, zone indexes with bit vector filters, in the context of row-oriented data warehouses.

In previous work, we presented the Group-Key Index, which implements an inverted index on the basis of the bit-packed value-id and showed that this index allows very fast lookups while introducing acceptable overhead to the partition-combining process [1].

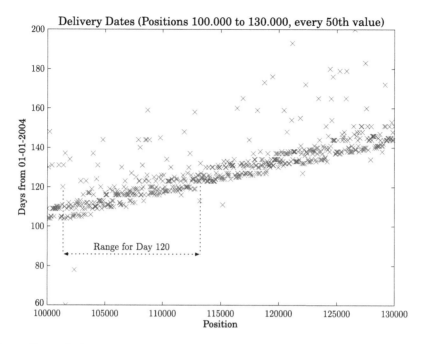

Fig. 1. Example for a strongly clustered column, showing delivery Dates from a productive ERP system. The values follow a general trend, but are not strictly ordered. The range for value 120 is given as an example.

2.2 Paper Structure and Contribution

In the following section we introduce our dictionary-compressed, bit-packed column storage scheme and the symbols that are used throughout the paper (Table 1). In Sect. 4 the Paged Index is presented. We explain its structure, give the memory traffic for a single lookup, and show the index rebuild algorithm. A size overview for exemplary configurations and the lookup algorithm is given as well. Afterwards, in Sect. 5, the column merge algorithm is shown, and extended in Sect. 6 to enable the index maintenance during the column merge process. In Sect. 7, we present the performance results for two index configurations. Findings and contributions are summed up in Sect. 9.

3   Bit-Packed Column Scan

We define the attribute vector $\mathbf{V}_\mathbf{M}^j$ to be a list of value-ids, referencing offsets in the sorted dictionary $\mathbf{U}_\mathbf{M}^j$ for column j. Values within $\mathbf{V}_\mathbf{M}^j$ are bit-packed with the minimal amount of bits necessary to reference the entries in $\mathbf{U}_\mathbf{M}^j$, we refer to the amount of bits with $\mathbf{E}_\mathbf{C}^j = \lceil \log_2(|\mathbf{U}_\mathbf{M}^j|) \rceil$ bits.

Consequently, to apply a predicate on a single column, the predicate conditions have to be translated into value-ids by performing a binary search on the

Table 1. Symbol definition. Entities annotated with ′ represent the merged (updated) entry.

Description	Unit	Symbol
Number of columns in the table	-	$\mathbf{N}_C$
Number of tuples in the main/delta partition	-	$\mathbf{N}_M, \mathbf{N}_D$
Number of tuples in the updated table	-	$\mathbf{N}'_M$
For a given column $j; j \in [1 \dots \mathbf{N}_C]$:		
Main/delta partition of the jth column	-	$\mathbf{M}^j, \mathbf{D}^j$
Merged column	-	$\mathbf{M}'^j$
Attribute vector of the jth column	-	$\mathbf{V}_M^j, \mathbf{V}_D^j$
Updated main attribute vector	-	$\mathbf{V}_M'^j$
Sorted dictionary of $\mathbf{M}^j / \mathbf{D}^j$	-	$\mathbf{U}_M^j, \mathbf{U}_D^j$
Updated main dictionary	-	$\mathbf{U}_M'^j$
CSB+ Tree Index on $\mathbf{D}^j$	-	$\mathbf{T}^j$
Compressed Value-Length	bits	$\mathbf{E}_C^j$
New Compressed Value-Length	bits	$\mathbf{E}_C'^j$
Length of Address in Main Partition	bits	$\mathbf{A}^j$
Fraction of unique values in $\mathbf{M}^j / \mathbf{D}^j$	-	λ_M^j, λ_D^j
Auxiliary structure for $\mathbf{M}^j / \mathbf{D}^j$	-	$\mathbf{X}_M^j, \mathbf{X}_D^j$
Paged Index	-	$\mathbf{I}_M^j$
Paged Index Pagesize	-	$\mathbf{P}^j$
Number of Pages	-	g
Memory Traffic	bytes	MT

main dictionary $\mathbf{U}_M^j$ and a scan of the main attribute vector $\mathbf{V}_M^j$. Of importance is here the scanning of $\mathbf{V}_M^j$, which involves the read of MT_{CS} bytes from main memory, as defined in Eq. 1.

$$MT_{CS} = \mathbf{N}_M \cdot \frac{\mathbf{E}_C^j}{8} = \mathbf{N}_M \cdot \frac{\lceil \log_2(|\mathbf{U}_M^j|) \rceil}{8} \text{ bytes} \qquad (1)$$

Inserts and updates to the compressed column are handled by a delta partition, thereby avoiding to re-encode the column for each insert [5]. The delta partition is stored uncompressed and extended by a CSB+ tree index to allow for fast lookups. If the delta partition reaches a certain threshold it is merged with the main partition. This process and the extension to update the Paged Index will be explained in detail in Sect. 5.

4   Paged Index

While indices in classic databases are well studied and researched, the increase of access speed to data for in-memory databases allows to rethink indexing techniques. Now, that the data in columnar in-memory stores can be accessed at the speed of RAM, it becomes possible to scan the complete column to evaluate queries - an operation that is prohibitively slow on disk for huge datasets (Fig. 2).

We propose the Paged Index, which benefits from clustered value distributions and focuses on reducing the memory traffic for the scan operation, while adding as little overhead as possible to the merge process for index maintenance. Additionally the index uses only minimal index storage space and is built for a mixed workload. Figure 1 shows an example of real ERP customer data, outlining delivery dates from a productive system. Clearly, the data follows a strong trend and consecutive values are only from a small value domain with a high spatial locality. Consequently, the idea behind a Paged Index is to partition a column into pages and to store bitmap indices for each value, reflecting in which pages the respective value occurs in. Therefore, scan operators only have to consider pages that are actually containing the value, which can drastically reduce the search space.

4.1   Index Structure

To use the Paged Index, the column is logically split into multiple equally sized pages. The last page is allowed to be of smaller size. Let the pagesize be $\mathbf{P}^j$, then

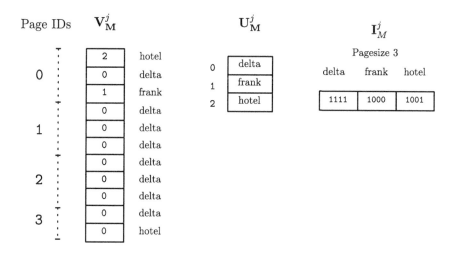

Fig. 2. An example of the Paged Index for $\mathbf{P}^j = 3$

$\mathbf{M}^j$ contains $g = \lceil \frac{\mathbf{N}_M}{\mathbf{P}^j} \rceil$ pages. For each of the encoded values in the dictionary $\mathbf{U}_M^j$ now a bitvector $\mathbf{B}_v^j$ is created, with v being the value-id of the encoded value, equal to its offset in $\mathbf{U}_M^j$. The bitvector contains exactly one bit for each page.

$$\mathbf{B}_v^j = (b_0, b_1...b_g) \tag{2}$$

Each bit in $\mathbf{B}_v^j$ marks whether value-id v can be found within the subrange represented by that page. To determine the actual tuple-id of the matching values, the according subrange has to be scanned. If b_x is set, one or more occurrences of the value-id can be found in the attribute vector between offset $x * \mathbf{P}^j$ (inclusive) and $(x+1) * \mathbf{P}^j$ (exclusive) as represented by Eq. 3. The Paged Index is the set of bitvectors for all value-ids, as defined in Eq. 4.

$$b_x \in \mathbf{B}_v^j : b_x = 1 \Leftrightarrow v \in \mathbf{V}_M^j[x \cdot \mathbf{P}^j...((x+1) \cdot \mathbf{P}^j - 1)] \tag{3}$$

$$I_M = \left[\mathbf{B}_0^j, \mathbf{B}_1^j, ..., \mathbf{B}_{|\mathbf{U}_M^j|-1}^j \right] \tag{4}$$

4.2 Index Size Estimate

The Paged Index is stored in one consecutive bitvector. For each distinct value and each page a bit is stored. The size in bits is given by Eq. 5. In Table 2 we show the resulting index sizes for some exemplary configurations.

$$\mathbf{s}(\mathbf{I}_M^j) = |\mathbf{U}_M^j| * \lceil \frac{\mathbf{N}_M}{\mathbf{P}^j} \rceil \text{ bits} \tag{5}$$

Table 2. Example sizes of the Paged Index

$\mathbf{N}_M$	$|\mathbf{U}_M^j|$	$\mathbf{P}^j$	$\mathbf{s}(\mathbf{I}_M^j)$	$\mathbf{s}(\mathbf{V}_M^j)$
100,000	10	4096	32 Byte	49 K
100,000	10	65536	3 Byte	49 K
100,000	100,000	4096	310 K	208 K
100,000	100,000	65536	31 K	208 K
1,000,000,000	10	4096	298 K	477 M
1,000,000,000	10	65536	19 K	477 M
1,000,000,000	100,000	4096	3 G	2 G
1,000,000,000	100,000	65536	182 M	2 G

4.3 Index Enabled Lookups

If no index is present to determine all tuple-ids for a single value-id, the attribute vector $\mathbf{V}_M^j$ is scanned from the beginning to the end and each compressed value-id is compared against the requested value-id. The resulting tuple-ids, which equal to the position in $\mathbf{V}_M^j$, are written to a dynamically allocated results vector. With the help of the Paged Index the scan costs can be minimized by evaluating only relevant parts of $\mathbf{V}_M^j$.

Algorithm 1. Scanning the Column with a Paged Index

1: **procedure** PAGEDINDEXSCAN (VALUEID)
2:    $bitsPerRun = \frac{|\mathbf{I}_M^j|}{|\mathbf{U}_M^j|}$
3:    $results = vector < uint >$
4:    **for** $page = 0; page \leq bitsPerRun; ++page$ **do**
5:        **if** $\mathbf{I}_M^j[bitsPerRun * valueid + page] == 1$ **then**
6:            $startOffset = page * \mathbf{P}^j$
7:            $endOffset = (page + 1) * \mathbf{P}^j$
8:            **for** $position = startOffset; position < endOffset; ++position$ **do**
9:                **if** $\mathbf{V}_M^j[position] == valueid$ **then**
10:                   $results.pushback(position)$
11:                **end if**
12:            **end for**
13:        **end if**
14:    **end for**
15:    return $results$
16: **end procedure**

Our evaluated implementation additionally decompresses multiple bit-packed values at once for maximum performance. Algorithm 1 shows the simplified implementation. The minimum memory traffic of an index-assisted partial scan of the attribute vector for a single value-id is given by Eq. 7.

$$minPagesPerDistinctValue = \left\lceil \frac{\mathbf{N}_M}{\mathbf{P}^j * |\mathbf{U}_M^j|} \right\rceil \qquad (6)$$

$$MT_{PagedIndex} = \left\lceil \frac{\mathbf{N}_M}{\mathbf{P}^j \cdot 8} \right\rceil + \left\lceil \frac{\mathbf{N}_M}{\mathbf{P}^j \cdot |\mathbf{U}_M^j|} \right\rceil \cdot \frac{\mathbf{P}^j \cdot \mathbf{E}_C^j}{8} \text{ bytes} \qquad (7)$$

4.4 Rebuild of the Index

To extent an existing compressed column with an index, the index has to be built. Additionally, a straightforward approach to enable index maintenance for the merge of the main and delta partition is to rebuild the index after a new, merged main partition has been created. Since all operations are in-memory, Rao et al. [8] claim that for bulk-operations an index rebuild is a viable choice. We take the rebuild as a baseline for further improvements.

5 Column Merge

Our in-memory column store maintains two partitions for each column: a read-optimized, compressed main partition and a writable delta partition. To allow for fast queries on the delta partition, it has to be kept small. To achieve this, the delta partition is merged with the main partition after its size has increased beyond a certain threshold. As explained in [5], the performance of this merge process is paramount to the overall sustainable insert performance. The inputs to the algorithm consists of the compressed main partition and the uncompressed delta partition with an CSB+ tree index [8]. The output is a new dictionary encoded main partition.

The algorithm is the basis for our index-aware merge process that will be presented in the next section.

We perform the merge using the following two steps:

1. **Merge Main Dictionary and Delta Index, Create value-ids for $\mathbf{D}^j$.**
   We simultaneously iterate over $\mathbf{U}_{\mathbf{M}}^j$ and the leafs of $\mathbf{T}^j$ and create the new sorted dictionary $\mathbf{U}_{\mathbf{M}}^{\prime j}$ and the auxiliary structure $\mathbf{X}_{\mathbf{M}}^j$. Because $\mathbf{T}^j$ contains a list of all positions for each distinct value in the delta partition of the column, we can set all positions in the value-id vector $\mathbf{V}_{\mathbf{D}}^j$. This leads to non-continuous access to $\mathbf{V}_{\mathbf{D}}^j$. Note that the value-ids in $\mathbf{V}_{\mathbf{D}}^j$ refer to the new dictionary $\mathbf{U}_{\mathbf{M}}^{\prime j}$.

2. **Create New Attribute Vector.** This step consists of creating the new main attribute vector $\mathbf{V}_{\mathbf{M}}^{\prime j}$ by concatenating the main and delta partition's attribute vectors $\mathbf{V}_{\mathbf{M}}^j$ and $\mathbf{V}_{\mathbf{D}}^j$. The compressed values in $\mathbf{V}_{\mathbf{M}}^j$ are updated by a lookup in the auxiliary structure $\mathbf{X}_{\mathbf{M}}^j$ as shown in Eq. 8. Values from $\mathbf{V}_{\mathbf{D}}^j$ are copied without translation to $\mathbf{V}_{\mathbf{M}}^{\prime j}$. The new attribute vector $\mathbf{V}_{\mathbf{M}}^{\prime j}$ will contain the correct offsets for the corresponding values in $\mathbf{U}_{\mathbf{M}}^{\prime j}$, by using $\mathbf{E}_C^{\prime j}$ bits-per-value, calculated as shown in Eq. 9.

$$\mathbf{V}_{\mathbf{M}}^{\prime j}[i] = \mathbf{V}_{\mathbf{M}}^j[i] + \mathbf{X}_{\mathbf{M}}^j[\mathbf{V}_{\mathbf{M}}^j[i]] \quad \forall i \in [0...\mathbf{N}_M - 1] \tag{8}$$

Algorithm 2. Rebuild of Paged Index

1: **procedure** REBUILD PAGED INDEX
2:      $bitsPerRun = \frac{\mathbf{N}_M + \mathbf{P}^j - 1}{\mathbf{P}^j}$
3:      $\mathbf{I}_M^j[0...(bitsPerRun * |\mathbf{U}_M^j|)] = 0$
4:      **for** $pos = 0; pos \leq \mathbf{N}_M; ++pos$ **do**
5:           $valueid = \mathbf{V}_M^j[pos]$
6:           $run = valueid * bitsPerRun$
7:           $page = \frac{pos}{\mathbf{P}^j}$
8:           $\mathbf{I}_M^j[run + page] = 1$
9:      **end for**
10: **end procedure**

Note that the optimal amount of bits-per-value for the bit-packed $\mathbf{V}_\mathbf{M}^{'j}$ can only be evaluated after the cardinality of $\mathbf{U}_\mathbf{M}^j \cup \mathbf{D}^j$ is determined. If we accept a non-optimal compression, we can set the compressed value length to the sum of the cardinalities of the dictionary $\mathbf{U}_\mathbf{M}^j$ and the delta CSB+ tree index $\mathbf{T}^j$. Since the delta partition is expected to be much smaller than the main partition, the difference from the optimal compression is low.

$$\mathbf{E}_C^{'j} = \lceil \log_2(|\mathbf{U}_\mathbf{M}^j \cup \mathbf{D}^j|) \rceil \leq \lceil \log_2(|\mathbf{U}_\mathbf{M}^j| + |\mathbf{T}^j|) \rceil \qquad (9)$$

Step 1's complexity is determined by the size of the union of the dictionaries and the size of the delta partition. Its complexity is $\mathcal{O}(|\mathbf{U}_\mathbf{M}^j \cup \mathbf{U}_\mathbf{D}^j| + |\mathbf{D}^j|)$. Step 2 is dependent on the length of the new attribute vector, $\mathcal{O}(\mathbf{N}_M + \mathbf{N}_D)$.

6   Index-Aware Column Merge

We now integrate the index rebuild into the column merge process. This allows us to reduce the memory traffic and create a more efficient algorithm to merge columns with a Paged Index.

Algorithm 3. Extended Dictionary Merge

1: **procedure** EXTENDEDDICTIONARYMERGE
2:     $d, m, n = 0$
3:     $g = \lceil \frac{\mathbf{N}_M}{\mathbf{P}^j} \rceil$ (Number of Pages)
4:     **while** $d \mathrel{!=} |\mathbf{T}^j|$ or $m \mathrel{!=} |\mathbf{U}_\mathbf{M}^j|$ **do**
5:         processM $= (\mathbf{U}_\mathbf{M}^j[m] <= \mathbf{T}^j[d]$ or $d == |\mathbf{T}^j|)$
6:         processD $= (\mathbf{T}^j[d] <= \mathbf{U}_\mathbf{M}^j[m]$ or $m == |\mathbf{U}_\mathbf{M}^j|)$
7:         **if** processM **then**
8:             $\mathbf{U}_\mathbf{M}^{'j}[n] \leftarrow \mathbf{U}_\mathbf{M}^j[m]$
9:             $\mathbf{X}_\mathbf{M}^j[m] \leftarrow n - m$
10:             $I'_M[n * g \cdots n * (g+1)] = I_M[m * g \cdots m(g+1)]$
11:             $m \leftarrow m + 1$
12:         **end if**
13:         **if** processD **then**
14:             $\mathbf{U}_\mathbf{M}^{'j}[n] \leftarrow \mathbf{T}^j[d]$
15:             **for** dpos in $\mathbf{T}^j[d].positions$ **do**
16:                 $\mathbf{V}_\mathbf{D}^{'j}[dpos] = n$
17:                 $I_M^{'j}[n * \frac{(|\mathbf{V}_\mathbf{M}^j| + |\mathbf{V}_\mathbf{D}^j|)}{\mathbf{P}^j} + \frac{|\mathbf{V}_\mathbf{M}^j| + dpos}{\mathbf{P}^j}] = 1$
18:             **end for**
19:             $d \leftarrow d + 1$
20:         **end if**
21:         $n \leftarrow n + 1$
22:     **end while**
23: **end procedure**

We extend Step 1 of the column merge process from Sect. 5 to maintain the Paged Index. During the dictionary merge we perform additional steps for each processed dictionary entry. The substeps are extended as follows:

1. **For Dictionary Entries from the Main Partition.** Calculate the begin and end offset in $\mathbf{I}_M^j$ and the starting offset in $\mathbf{I}_M^{j'}$. Copy the range from $\mathbf{I}_M^j$ to $\mathbf{I}_M^{j'}$. The additional bits in the run are left zero, because the value is not present in the delta partition.
2. **For CSB+ Index Entries from the Delta Partition.** Calculate the position of the run in $\mathbf{I}_M^{j'}$, read all positions from $\mathbf{T}^j$, increase them by $\mathbf{N}_M$, and set the according bits in $\mathbf{I}_M^{j'}$.
3. **Entries found in both Partitions.** Perform both steps sequentially.

Algorithm 3 shows a modified dictionary merge algorithm to maintain the paged index during the column merge.

7   Evaluation

We evaluate our Paged Index on a clustered column. In a clustered column equal data entries are grouped together, but the column is not necessarily sorted by the value. Our index does perform best, if each value's occurrences form exactly one group, however it is not required. Outliers or multiple groups are supported by the Paged Index.

With the help of the index the column scan is accelerated by scanning only the pages which are known to have at least one occurrence of the desired value.

The benchmarks were performed on a two socket Intel Xeon X5650 system with 48 GB of RAM. In Fig. 3 the CPU cycles for the column scan and two configurations of the Paged Index are shown. We choose pagesizes of 4096 and 16384 entries as an example. The Paged Index enables an performance increase of two orders of magnitude for columns with a medium to high amount of distinct values through a drastic reduction of of the search scope. For smaller dictionaries,

Table 3. Example sizes of the evaluated Paged Index

$\mathbf{N}_M$	$|\mathbf{U}_M^j|$	$\mathbf{P}^j$	$s(\mathbf{I}_M^j)$	$s(\mathbf{V}_M^j)$
3,000,000	10	4096	917 byte	1.4 M
3,000,000	10	65536	58 byte	1.4 M
3,000,000	100,000	4096	8.7 M	6.1 M
3,000,000	100,000	65536	571.0 K	6.1 M
3,000,000	1,000,000	4096	87.4 M	7.2 M
3,000,000	1,000,000	65536	5.6 M	7.2 M
3,000,000	3,000,000	4096	262.3 M	7.9 M
3,000,000	3,000,000	65536	16.7 M	7.9 M

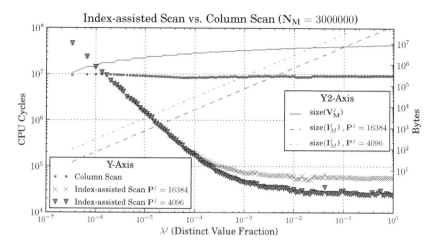

Fig. 3. Scan performance and index sizes in comparison

the benefit is lower. However an order of magnitude is already reached with $\lambda^j = 10^{-5}$, which corresponds to 30 distinct values in our example. For very small dictionaries with less than 5 values, the overhead of reading the Paged Index leads to a performance decrease. In these cases the Paged Index should not be applied to a column. In Table 3 the index and attribute vector sizes for some of the measured configurations are given. The Paged Index can deliver its performance increase for columns with a medium amount of distinct values for only little storage overhead. For the columns with a very high distinct value count the Paged Index grows prohibitively large. Note, that the storage footprint halves by each doubling of the pagesize. For the aforementioned delivery dates column the Paged Index decreases the scan time for a specific value-id by a factor 20.

8   Future Work

The current design of a bit-packed attribute vector does not allow a fixed mapping of the resulting sub-ranges to memory pages. In future work we want to compare the performance benefits if a attribute vector is designed, so that the reading of a sub-range leads to at most one transaction lookaside buffer (TLB) miss.

Other interesting topics include the automatic determination of the best page size, index compression and varying page sizes.

9   Conclusion

Shifted access speeds in main memory databases and special domain knowledge in enterprise systems allow for a reevaluation of indexing concepts. With the original data available at the speed of main memory, indices do not need to narrow down the search scope as far as in disk based databases. Therefore, relatively small indices can have huge impacts, especially if they are designed towards a specific data distribution.

In this paper, we proposed the Paged Index, which is tailored towards columns with clustered data. As our analyses of real customer data showed, such data distributions are especially common in enterprise systems. By indexing the occurrence of values on a block level, the search scope for scan operations can be reduced drastically with the use of a Paged Index. In our experimental evaluation, we report speed improvements up to two orders of magnitude, while only adding little overhead for the index maintenance and storage. Finally, we proposed an integration of the index maintenance into the merge process, further reducing index maintenance costs.

References

1. Faust, M., Schwalb, D., Krueger, J., Plattner, H.: Fast lookups for in-memory column stores: Group-key indices, lookup and maintenance. In: ADMS'2012, pp. 13–22 (2012)
2. Graefe, G.: Fast loads and fast queries. In: Pedersen, T.B., Mohania, M.K., Tjoa, A.M. (eds.) DaWaK 2009. LNCS, vol. 5691, pp. 111–124. Springer, Heidelberg (2009)
3. Grund, M., Krueger, J., Plattner, H., Zeier, A., Cudre-Mauroux, P., Madden, S.: HYRISE-a main memory hybrid storage engine. Proc. VLDB Endowment 4(2), 105–116 (2010)
4. Idreos, S., Manegold, S., Kuno, H., Graefe, G.: Merging what's cracked, cracking what's merged: adaptive indexing in main-memory column-stores. Proc. VLDB Endowment 4(9), 586–597 (2011)
5. Krueger, J., Kim, C., Grund, M., Satish, N., Schwalb, D., Chhugani, J., Plattner, H., Dubey, P., Zeier, A.: Fast updates on read-optimized databases using multi-core CPUs. Proc. VLDB Endowment 5(1), 61–72 (2011)
6. Plattner, H.: A common database approach for OLTP and OLAP using an in-memory column database. In: SIGMOD '09 Proceedings of the 2009 ACM SIGMOD International Conference on Management of data, pp. 1–8 (2009)
7. Plattner, H., Zeier, A.: In-Memory Data Management: An Inflection Point for Enterprise Applications. Springer, Heidelberg (2011)
8. Rao, J., Ross, K.: Cache conscious indexing for decision-support in main memory. In: Proceedings of the International Conference on Very Large Data Bases (VLDB), pp. 78–89 (1999)
9. SAP-AG. The SAP HANA database-an architecture overview. Data Engineering (2012)
10. Stonebraker, M., Abadi, D., Batkin, A., Chen, X., Cherniack, M., Ferreira, M., Lau, E., Lin, A., Madden, S., O'Neil, E.: C-store: a column-oriented DBMS. In: Proceedings of the 31st International Conference on Very large data bases, pp. 553–564 (2005)

11. Willhalm, T., Popovici, N., Boshmaf, Y., Plattner, H., Zeier, A., Schaffner, J.: SIMD-scan: ultra fast in-memory table scan using on-chip vector processing units. Proc. VLDB Endowment **2**(1), 385–394 (2009)
12. Zukowski, M., Boncz, P., Nes, N., Heman, S.: MonetDB/X100-A DBMS in the CPU cache. IEEE Data Eng. Bull. **28**(2), 17–22 (2005)

Compiled Plans for In-Memory Path-Counting Queries

Brandon Myers$^{(\boxtimes)}$, Jeremy Hyrkas, Daniel Halperin, and Bill Howe

Department of Computer Science and Engineering,
University of Washington, Seattle, WA, USA
{bdmyers,hyrkas,dhalperi,billhowe}@cs.washington.edu

Abstract. Dissatisfaction with relational databases for large-scale graph processing has motivated a new class of graph databases that offer fast graph processing but sacrifice the ability to express basic relational idioms. However, we hypothesize that the performance benefits amount to implementation details, not a fundamental limitation of the relational model. To evaluate this hypothesis, we are exploring code-generation to produce fast in-memory algorithms and data structures for graph patterns that are inaccessible to conventional relational optimizers.

In this paper, we present preliminary results for this approach on path-counting queries, which includes triangle counting as a special case. We compile Datalog queries into main-memory pipelined hash-join plans in C++, and show that the resulting programs easily outperform PostgreSQL on real graphs with different degrees of skew. We then produce analogous parallel programs for Grappa, a runtime system for distributed memory architectures. Grappa is a good target for building a parallel query system as its shared memory programming model and communication mechanisms provide productivity and performance when building communication-intensive applications. Our experiments suggest that Grappa programs using hash joins have competitive performance with queries executed on a commercial parallel database. We find preliminary evidence that a code generation approach simplifies the design of a query engine for graph analysis and improves performance over conventional relational databases.

1 Introduction

Increased interest in the analysis of large-scale graphs found in social networking, web analytics, and bioinformatics has led to the development of a number of graph processing systems [1, 23]. These specialized systems have been developed, in part, because relational DBMSs are perceived as being too slow for graph algorithms. These systems thus sacrifice full relational algebra support in favor of improved performance for graph tasks. However, realistic applications typically involve relations as well as graphs—e.g., Facebook's content is richer than just its friend network—suggesting that relational models and languages should not be completely abandoned.

© Springer International Publishing Switzerland 2015
A. Jagatheesan et al. (Eds.): IMDM 2013/2014, LNCS 8921, pp. 28–43, 2015.
DOI: 10.1007/978-3-319-13960-9_3

As a logical data model, relations arguably subsume graphs. Every graph can be trivially represented as an edge relation, but even simple relational schemas must be transformed in non-trivial ways to "shred" them into graphs. Consider a relation Order(customer,part,supplier). Each tuple in this relation is a hyper-edge relating a particular customer, a particular part, and a particular supplier. To represent a tuple (c, p, s) as part of a graph, three edges (c, p), (p, s), (s, c) must be represented and exposed to the user for manipulation in queries. As another example, consider two relations Friend(person1, person2) and Sibling(person1, person2). A natural graph representation would create one edge for each tuple in Friend and one edge for each tuple in Sibling. But to distinguish friends from siblings, each edge needs to be labeled. Besides increasing the space complexity, this extra label must be manipulated by the user explicitly in queries.

So perhaps the relational model is preferable as a logical interface to the data, but the value proposition of graph databases is typically performance. By using specialized data structures and algorithms and operating primarily in main memory, these systems can outperform relational databases at graph-oriented tasks. However, we hypothesize that these specializations are essentially implementation details, and that there is no fundamental reason that a relational engine could not exploit them when appropriate.

To test this idea, we use code generation to produce fast in-memory query plans for simple graph pattern queries, in two contexts. First, we generate pipelined query plans over associative data structures in C++ and show that these programs significantly outperform tuned and indexed RDBMS implementations. Second, we show how analogous query plans targeting a parallel computation framework called Grappa can compete with a tuned and indexed MPP database.

In our experiments, we consider a class of *path-counting* queries (defined precisely in Sect. 3), which includes triangle counting [24] as a special case. These queries arise in both graph and relational contexts, including in credibility algorithms for detecting spam [6] and in probabilistic algorithms [30]. To handle "hybrid" graph-relational applications, we retain the relational data model and a relational query language—Datalog.

While only non-recursive queries are explored in this paper, Datalog with recursion will be targeted in future experiments.

Our approach is inspired by other work in compiling relational algebra expressions and SQL queries [20], but our goal is different. We wish to support a variety of back-end runtime systems and explore various algorithms for specific graph patterns, rather than generate the fastest possible machine code for individual relational operator algorithms.

For parallel evaluation, we are concerned with the competing factors of scaling up: distributing data allows for higher bandwidth access but greater network usage amidst random access. For workloads with irregular memory access, like that in sequences of hash joins, high throughput can be achieved in modern processors given sufficient concurrency [18]. With this observation in mind, we employ a novel parallel runtime system, Grappa [19], designed for irregular workloads. Grappa targets commodity clusters but exposes a partitioned global address space to the programmer. This abstraction allows us to write code that is structurally similar to that of our serial C++ runtime, while allowing our algorithms and the Grappa engine to apply optimizations that exploit locality.

The contributions of this paper are:

1. A code generator that translates path-counting queries expressed in Datalog into fast C++ programs that implement join-based query plans over associative data structures.
2. In-memory algorithms for parallel path-counting queries in Grappa, along with generic templates compatible with our code generation framework.
3. Experimental results comparing generated C++ programs against the serial relational database PostgreSQL, showing the generated plans to be 3.5×–7.5× faster than tuned and optimized relational query plans.
4. Experimental results comparing path-counting queries in Grappa to the Greenplum commercial parallel RDBMS.

In the next section, we briefly describe the Grappa parallel framework that we use as a compilation target for parallel plans. In Sect. 3, we describe our code generation approach and evaluate the performance of the resulting plans in Sect. 4.

2   Grappa: Programming for Irregular Applications

Grappa is a C++11 runtime for commodity clusters that is designed to provide high performance for massively parallel *irregular* applications, which are characterized by unpredictable access patterns, poor locality, and data skew. In these situations, communication costs dominate runtime for two reasons: random access to large data does not utilize caches and commodity networks are not designed for small messages. Interconnects like Ethernet are InfiniBand are designed to achieve maximum bisection bandwidth for packet sizes of 10 KB–1 MB, while irregular accesses may be on the order of 64 bytes—the size of a typical cache line.

- a **partitioned global address space** (PGAS) to enable programmer productivity without hindering the ability to optimize performance for NUMA shared memory and distributed memory systems
- **task and parallel loop constructs** for expressing abundant concurrency
- **fine-grained synchronization and active messages** to allow for asynchronous execution and low cost atomic operations, respectively
- **lightweight multithreading** to provide fast context switching between tasks
- a **buffering communication layer** that combines messages with the same destination to utilize the network better than fine-grained messages
- **distributed dynamic load balancing** to cope with dynamic task imbalance in a scalable way

Grappa provides an appropriate level of abstraction as a target platform for our query compilation approach. The global address space allows us to generate relatively simple code, and parallel loop constructs preclude the need to emit explicitly-multi-threaded routines. However, Grappa is sufficiently expressive to allow us to optimize for locality, and we can use lower-level communication abstractions to build distributed algorithms for special situations.

Concurrency can be expressed with a variety of arbitrarily nestable parallel loop constructs that exploit spatial locality when it exists; these idioms are a natural fit for pipelined query plans.

3   Code Generation for Path-Counting Queries

Following Seo, Guo, and Lam [26], we adopt a Datalog syntax for expressing graph queries. In this paper, we show only preliminary results of the efficacy of the code generation approach rather than a full Datalog implementation.

We focus on *path-counting queries*, of which triangle counting is a special case. Each query is of the form

$$\gamma_{count}(\sigma_c(\sigma_1 R_1 \bowtie \sigma_2 R_2 \bowtie \ldots \bowtie \sigma_N R_N)) \tag{1}$$

where γ is an aggregation operator for counting the final results. The extra selection operator σ_c can enforce relationships between non-adjacent vertices in the path. In particular, this condition can enforce that the path form a cycle, as in the triangle queries. Each leaf and each internal node in the plan may be filtered by a select operator. The internal selection conditions allow us to express, for example, a triangle counting query (see below). The count operation may optionally remove duplicates before counting, which results in significantly different performance in all tested systems.

We consider a graph represented as a relation with the schema (`src:int`, `dst:int`). Additional attributes are allowed, but are not considered in these preliminary experiments. Each tuple (a, b) represents an outgoing edge from vertex a to vertex b. While a table is not the most memory efficient way of representing a graph [26], it allows us to easily apply concepts of relational algebra to the graph problems presented.

Through the lens of relational algebra, paths in a graph are expressed as a series of joins on the edge relations. For example, the two-hops (or friends of friends) query is a single join on the *edges* table [15]. In Datalog, this query is expressed as

```
Twohop(s,d)  :- edges(s,m), edges(m,d).
```

A three-hop query would add one additional join to the query above. A popular case of the three-hop query in large graphs is triangle counting [12,22], where a triangle must be a cycle. Triangles in a graph represent a three-hop where the source s and destination d are the same vertex. In Datalog, directed triangles are expressed as:

```
Triangle(x,y,z)  :- edges(x,y), edges(y,z),
                    edges(z,x), x < y, y < z.
```

The final conditions in the Datalog rule ensure that directed triangles are only counted once, instead of three times (i.e. $1, 2, 3$ is counted, but $3, 1, 2$ is not). These conditions correspond to selects in relational algebra.

3.1   Generating Code from Datalog

To generate implementations of path-counting queries, we constructed a query compilation framework that can produce pipelined query plans over associative data structures. The overall structure is similar to a typical relational plan, but the use of nested data structures admits some algorithmic improvements that are relatively simple but difficult for typical optimizers to exploit, as we will see. The input is a graph query written in Datalog, and the output is imperative source code. The compiler is written in Python using the NetworkX package [10] for manipulating the query graph. Each rule in the source program[1] is converted to a logical relational algebra expression and then to a physical plan.

In general, a path of k edges through a graph involves $k - 1$ self-joins on the *edges* relation. To avoid the cost of constructing the results of each join in memory for the next join, we emit pipelined plan consisting of a series of nested hash-joins: a lookup table (tree-based rather than a hash-based; see Sect. 3.2) is constructed over the join column for the left relation, and then probed with tuples from the right relation. Pseudocode plans for the two-hop and triangle queries appear in Figs. 1 and 2 respectively, along with each query's relational plan.

The two-hop query explored in this paper requires duplicate elimination, as there may be multiple paths from vertex s to vertex d. We perform duplicate elimination by inserting results into a set data structure. Since the start vertex is unique for all paths from k, we can optimize the memory usage by logically grouping by start vertex and iterating through the groups one at a time. This optimization reduces the worst case size of the set by $O(|V|)$. The improvement in lookup time yielded a 5× decrease in runtime for two-hop on the datasets in our experiments. Consequently, whenever a query requires a distinct variable from the outer relation, we perform a group-by on the outer relation. This technique is a scheduling optimization, the motivation for which is similar to that of depth-first search: by exploring all paths from s first, we can reduce memory utilization. We believe this type of custom optimization is a perfect fit for a code generation technique; as new patterns are recognized, the known optimal code for that pattern of query can be automatically generated. This gives our code generation approach potential to generate algorithms that are traditionally not considered by relational DBMS optimizers (such as algorithms used by graph databases), as well as algorithms that are more efficient than those of graph databases. Pseudocode for the distinct source-destination optimization is shown in Fig. 1.

---

[1] All queries considered in this paper can be expressed with a single Datalog rule.

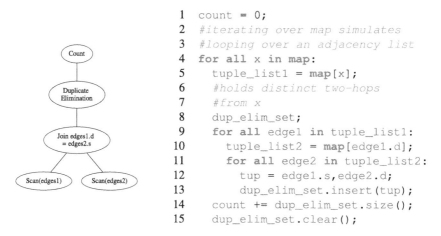

```
1   count = 0;
2   #iterating over map simulates
3   #looping over an adjacency list
4   for all x in map:
5     tuple_list1 = map[x];
6     #holds distinct two-hops
7     #from x
8     dup_elim_set;
9     for all edge1 in tuple_list1:
10      tuple_list2 = map[edge1.d];
11      for all edge2 in tuple_list2:
12        tup = edge1.s,edge2.d;
13        dup_elim_set.insert(tup);
14    count += dup_elim_set.size();
15    dup_elim_set.clear();
```

Fig. 1. Relational algebra and pseudocode for the distinct two-hop query. In the code on the right, the map variable maps each vertex x to all edges (x, y). The outer loop behaves as a relational group-by, and the set for duplicate elimination is moved inside the group-by (line 8) and cleared after each iteration (line 15). This approach allows for for better memory-usage.

3.2   C++ Code Generation

The first language targeted by our code generation model is C++. The logic for generating code described in Sect. 3.1 remains unchanged, but there are some language specific features. For example, in our C++ code, the "hash" table is an STL **map**. Similarly, duplicate elimination is performed by inserting results into an STL **set**. Both associative data structures are implemented with a red-black tree, but in experiments this was never a performance factor.

As tuples are scanned from disk, they are converted to structs and inserted into an STL **vector**. Each relation is scanned only once, regardless of how many times it appears in the query. Query processing then proceeds as described in Sect. 3.1.

End to end, this compiler allowed us to generate C++ code for path-counting queries from Datalog. Queries without grouping (such as the triangle query) generate code similar to the code shown above. Path queries requiring a distinct source and destination were generated using a "distinct mode", with a group-by structure as shown in Sect. 3.1. In Sect. 6, we discuss compiler extensions to support more general graph queries.

3.3   Queries in Grappa

Recall that Grappa provides a global address space and parallel for loop constructs. Each relation is scanned and loaded into an array, which Grappa distributes by default in a block-cyclic fashion.

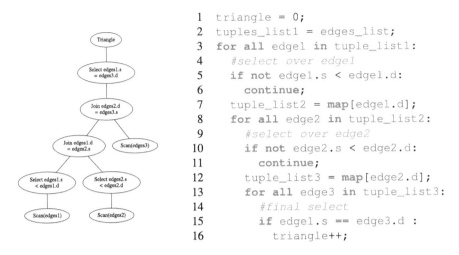

```
1   triangle = 0;
2   tuples_list1 = edges_list;
3   for all edge1 in tuple_list1:
4       #select over edge1
5       if not edge1.s < edge1.d:
6           continue;
7       tuple_list2 = map[edge1.d];
8       for all edge2 in tuple_list2:
9           #select over edge2
10          if not edge2.s < edge2.d:
11              continue;
12          tuple_list3 = map[edge2.d];
13          for all edge3 in tuple_list3:
14              #final select
15              if edge1.s == edge3.d :
16                  triangle++;
```

Fig. 2. Relational algebra and pseudocode for the triangle query. The select conditions for *edges2*, *edges2*, and the final *edges1.s = edges3.d* are shown in lines 5, 10, and 15. We note that in this example, more efficient code could be generated by pushing the selection conditions in lines 5 and 10 into the construction of the hash maps used in the join operations.

To compute a hash join, the build relation is hashed on the join key and used to populate a distributed hash table. The hash table representation is essentially equivalent to an adjacency list representation used in graph systems, but general enough to support arbitrary relations. This point is important: it is not obvious that there is a fundamental difference between a join-based evaluation approach and a graph-traversal approach. To compute a chain of joins, we use Grappa's abstractions for shared memory and parallel for-loops to produce nested, pipelined plans that are analogous to the serial case.

The parallel execution strategy for the nested parallel for-loops of a single pipeline is handled by the runtime system. Grappa uses recursive decomposition to spawn tasks for loop iterations and schedules them in depth-first order to use memory only linear in the number of threads. This approach is inspired by Cilk [5], but in Grappa the number of "threads" is determined by the number of concurrent tasks required to tolerate the latency to access distributed memory. Grappa's parallel for-loop mechanism supports different levels of granularity—that is, the number of consecutive loop-body iterations that each task executes. Currently, the level of granularity is fixed at compile time, but we expect that dynamic adjustments will be an important defense against unpredictable result sizes.

To exploit inter-pipeline parallelism, generated code spawns each pipeline as a separate task. No synchronization is required between independent sub-plans, but for joins, probes of the hash table block until the build phase is complete.

The `HashMultiMap` and `HashSet` used for joins and duplicate elimination are designed similarly to typical shared memory implementations, except the data structures are distributed. The entry point is a single shared array of buckets distributed block-cyclically across all cores in the cluster.

The critical part of our shared memory lookup structures for Grappa is how concurrent `insert` and `lookup` are implemented efficiently. By ensuring that a given `insert` or `lookup` touches only data localized to a single bucket, we can implement these operations as active messages. Grappa can mitigate skew by putting all edge lists in one block-cyclic distributed array as in compressed sparse row format, but in the experiments for this paper, we use a data structure that puts each edge list entirely on one machine. All operations on a given bucket are performed atomically, by the simple fact that each core has exclusive access to its local memory. This example shows how Grappa's partitioning of the global address space admits locality-aware optimizations.

Since Grappa uses multithreading to tolerate random access latency to distributed memory, execution flow of hash join probes looks similar to the explicit prefetching schemes by Chen et al. [7]. Specifically, prefetching a collection of independent hash buckets before performing loads is analogous to how Grappa switches out a thread on a remote memory operation.

Since the insertion for duplicate elimination is the last operation in the probing pipeline, the task does not need to block waiting for the insertion to complete, saving an extra context switch. We found that this optimization reduces the cost of duplicate elimination in Grappa by roughly 2× relative to using blocking inserts, which contributes to the particularly good performance of Grappa code for the two-hop query (see Sect. 4.4). This technique generalizes to continuation passing optimizations for certain types of queries, which is a subject for future work.

4   Evaluation

As a first step in studying our approach, we want to answer two questions experimentally. First, does our generated C++ code significantly outperform traditional DBMSs? Second, is Grappa an effective platform for parallel path query execution even without clever partitioning and other customizations for this task?

To answer these questions, we executed path queries to count distinct two-hop paths and triangles in standard public graph datasets. For the first question, we compared our generated C++ queries to PostgreSQL, a well-studied DBMS. Though the PostgreSQL installation was heavily indexed and our C++ code read non-indexed data from disk, our C++ code generated from Datalog was 3.5×–5× faster on a more skewed data set and 5×–7.5× faster on a less skewed data set.

For the second question, we compared Grappa with Greenplum, a commercial parallel DBMS. We evaluated Grappa on clusters comprising 2 to 64 nodes and an 8-node Greenplum installation. Without making any modifications to Grappa

Table 1. Salient properties of the graphs studied

Dataset	# Vertices (M)	# Edges (M)	# Distinct 2-hop paths	# Triangles
BSN	0.685	7.60	78 350 597	6 935 709
Twitter subset	0.166	4.53	1 056 317 985	14 912 950
com-livejournal	4.00	34.7	735 398 579	—
soc-livejournal	4.85	69.0	—	112 319 229

to support our application, the 8-node Grappa cluster completed queries as fast or faster than the 8-node Greenplum cluster, and scaled well to 32 nodes. We also found that Grappa's good performance extended across datasets and queries.

4.1 Datasets

We used standard, public graph datasets for our evaluations: the Berkeley-Stanford Network (BSN) graph [14]; a subset of the Twitter follower graph [13]; and two SNAP LiveJournal graphs [4,29]. We summarize salient properties of these graphs in Table 1. The Twitter subset is notable for its significant skew, leading to large intermediate results (discussed in Sect. 4.3). We evaluate the following queries.

4.2 Test Queries

In this paper, we are concerned primarily with relational, in-core execution techniques for graph-based tasks. We thus choose our queries and datasets to exercise these design points, namely choosing queries that will fit in the system memory but that are large enough to expose parallelism.

Two-path: count the number of distinct pairs (x, z) such that vertex x has a path of length two to z through any vertex y.

```
select count(*) from (select distinct a.src,b.dst from
    edges a, edges b where a.dst = b.src) z;
```

Triangle: count the number of ordered triangles in the graph.

```
select count(*) from edges a, edges b, edges c where a.src <
    a.dst and a.dst = b.src and b.src < b.dst and b.dst = c.
    src and c.dst = a.src;
```

A **variant three-path** query was also used to test the performance of queries involving multiple graph relations. For these experiments, the BSN and Twitter data sets were split into two disjoint relations, the larger of which contains roughly 90 % of the original edges. The first hop is taken in the smaller relation, then the intermediate results are joined to the larger relation.

4.3   Single-Node Experiments: C++ vs. PostgreSQL

We compared the generated C++ code against SQL queries in an indexed relational implementation using PostgreSQL.

All tests were performed on a shared-memory system running Linux kernel 2.6.32. The machine has 0.5 TB of main memory and 4 sockets, each with a 2.0 GHz, 12-core AMD Magny-cours processor. After code generation, the resulting C++ code was compiled using GCC 4.7 with -O3 optimization.

PostgreSQL 8.4 was configured to use 64 GB of shared buffer space and 50 GB of working memory. Indexes were created on both the *src* and *dst* variables of the *edges* relation, and then *edges* was clustered on the *src* variable. These optimizations were applied in an attempt to minimize the runtime for the queries. For all three plans, the query optimizer chose to execute a sort-merge join. For the two path query, the table is already sorted by *src*, so one instance of the *edges* relation is sorted by *dst*, and a standard sort-merge join was performed. In the case of triangle and three path, the intermediate result from the first join was sorted on *b.dst*, and then a sort-merge join was performed between the intermediate result and *c*. For comparison, we reran the PostgreSQL experiments with sort-merge joins disabled; the resulting plans used a hash-join, like our code, but were slower than the original plans.

Figures 3 and 4 show the runtime comparison of the two -path, three-path, and triangle queries for C++ vs. PostgreSQL on the BSN and Twitter graphs. Our automatically generated C++ code runs 3.5×–5× faster than PostgreSQL on the twitter data set and 5×–7.5× faster on the BSN data set.

Queries on the Twitter graph were slower because they resulted in many more results (Table 1). The key insight is that Twitter has both larger average degree (27 vs 11) and more vertices with both large in-degree and out-degree. The maximum out-degree in Twitter is 20 383, two orders of magnitude greater than the BSN graph. These properties of the Twitter graph cause the intermediate results of self-joins to be orders of magnitude larger than in the BSN graph, and indeed we see that Twitter has 13× as many two-paths.

The triangle query on a given data set is always faster than distinct two-hop, despite having larger intermediate join results—the extra join results in an order of magnitude more results than both two-hop and variant three-hop. The

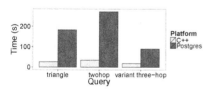

Fig. 3. Runtimes for the distinct two-hop, triangle, and variant three-hop queries on the BSN graph

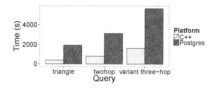

Fig. 4. Runtimes for the distinct two-hop, triangle and variant three-hop queries on the Twitter subset

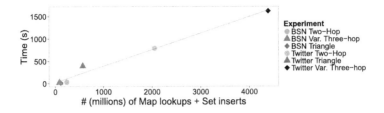

Fig. 5. There is a correlation between the sum of `map` lookups and `set` inserts and the runtime of the query generated as C++.

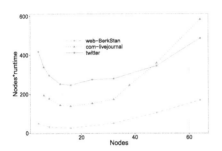
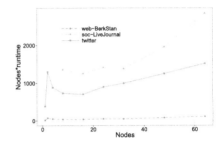

Fig. 6. Two-hop scalability on Grappa   **Fig. 7.** Triangle scalability on Grappa

reason is that the most costly step in the computation is duplicate elimination. Indeed, when we counted the number of operations used to implement duplicate elimination (map lookups and set inserts), we found a strong correlation with the runtime of the program (Fig. 5), reinforcing that duplicate elimination dominates costs.

4.4 Parallel Experiments: Grappa and Greenplum

We evaluate the scalability of Grappa and compare absolute performance that of Greenplum [27], a commercial parallel DBMS. To scale to larger systems, we used the same queries as above and extend to bigger datasets. For each dataset and query, we compare the runtime as we scale up the number of machines.

As Grappa is a research system for which we are still determining the best optimization strategies, we did not generate the Grappa code automatically. Instead, the query was manually coded in a style that is essentially isomorphic to the serial case.

We run the Grappa queries on allocations of a 144-node cluster of AMD Interlagos processors. Nodes have 32 cores (16 full datapaths) running at 2.1-GHz in two sockets, 64 GB of RAM, and 40-Gb Mellanox ConnectX-2 InfiniBand network cards. Nodes are connected via a QLogic InfiniBand switch.

Due to time and administration constraints, the Greenplum installation runs on a different system: an 8-node cluster of 2.0-GHz, 8-core Intel Xeon processors with 16 GB of RAM. Although setup this does not provide an apples-to-apples comparison between the two systems, we can still provide some context for the performance of Grappa queries. Greenplum database was tuned to utilize as much memory as possible and configured to use 2 segments per node. We show the best results between Greenplum partitions on *src*, *dst*, or *random* (although all runtimes were within about 10 %).

First, we examine the parallel efficiency of the queries implemented on Grappa. Figures 6 and 7 illustrate scalability using the metric of number of nodes multiplied by the runtime. With perfect scaling, this line would be flat (as doubling the number of cores would halve the runtime). Increasing values indicate suboptimal scaling.

On both queries, going from one node to two nodes incurs a performance penalty, as memory references must now go over the network. Four nodes is sufficient to gain back performance with parallelism. Two-hop on the Twitter subset scales well and runs in as little as 6.5s with 64 nodes. Most of the time is spent on insertions into the distinct set of results. For the other datasets, two-hop performance does not scale well beyond 32 nodes; in fact, for this query it degrades. Because 32 nodes utilizes all the data parallelism in these two datasets, the rising cost of set inserts over the network outweighs having more aggregate memory bandwidth. On triangles, Grappa scales well up to 32 nodes on com-livejournal and BSN but less efficiently on Twitter.

Unique among the systems studied, Grappa performs better on two-hop than on triangles. This improvement is not surprising, because Grappa is designed for high throughput random access, which occurs in hash insertions. Although context switches are fast, eliminating them in the inner loop can increase performance. Triangles requires more of them: one path through the triangles pipeline requires a task to do two blocking lookups (joins), while one path through the two-hop pipeline requires a task to do just one blocking lookup (join) and one non-blocking insert (distinct). Since set insertions are *fire-and-forget* and the inner loop of triangles contains no remote memory operations, setting the parallel granularity of the inner loop to be large (around 128) gave the best performance.

In Table 2, we list results for Greenplum and Grappa. These results were collected on different machines and networks; however, they indicate that graph path queries compiled to Grappa have the potential to be competitive with a commercial parallel RDBMS, especially in the case of duplicate elimination. To get an indication of the parallel performance of a single shared memory node using our code generation, we also wrote the triangle query by augmenting the generated C++ code with OpenMP pragmas. Shown is the best result with 16 cores, tuned to use dynamic scheduling on the outer two loops and guided scheduling with a chunk size of 8 on the inner loop. Due to additional overhead to share memory between cores in Grappa, for a single node, Grappa's performance with 16 cores equals that of 4 cores in OpenMP.

Table 2. Performance of code manually written for Grappa and OpenMP according to our generation technique and SQL queries on Greenplum

System	# Nodes	Query	Dataset	Runtime
Greenplum	8	two-hop distinct	com-livejournal	265.5 s
Grappa	8	two-hop distinct	com-livejournal	24.0 s
Grappa	32	two-hop distinct	com-livejournal	5.3 s
Greenplum	8	triangle	Twitter	84.3 s
Grappa	8	triangle	Twitter	91.6 s
Grappa	64	triangle	Twitter	24.0 s
OpenMP	1	triangle	Twitter	110.8 s

5   Related Work

DBToaster [2] compiles C++ code from SQL queries for fast delta processing for the view maintenance problem. More generally, Neumann compiles TPC-H style analytics queries to LLVM bytecode and C [20] using a typical iterator framework. In contrast, we seek specialized algorithms for specific graph query patterns.

Vertex-centric programming models including Pregel [17] and GraphLab [9] have become popular for graph computations. GraphLab supports asynchronous computation and prioritized scheduling, but offers no declarative query interface and cannot express simple relational idioms. By making Grappa one of our compiler targets, we can also support asynchronous execution.

Neo4j [1] is a graph database, with its own data model and graph query language. Unlike Grappa, the entire graph is replicated on all compute nodes, so it cannot scale to large graphs. Recent work has shown that SQL DBMSs can compete with graph databases for real world network datasets and shortest path queries [28].

SPARQL is a pattern language for graphs represented as a set of (subject, predicate, object) triples. A number of systems have focused on executing and optimizing SPARQL queries [8, 21], but we find SPARQL to be neither necessary nor sufficient for graph manipulation: Datalog is strictly more expressive than SPARQL without v1.1 path expressions [3], and the semantics of path expressions make query processing intractable [16].

Parallel databases like Greenplum are like conventional relational DBMSs but parallelize individual queries across shared-nothing architectures. Vertica [11] is a parallel DBMS designed for analytics and includes just-in-time compilation techniques. Grappa provides shared memory, as well as active messages, to the database system programmer. Since we are concerned with in-memory execution, we are exploring compiling rather than interpreting queries.

6 Future Work

We have focused on only a narrow class of path-counting queries; we plan to extend the framework to handle full Datalog. This allows for a much larger scope of graph queries, such as conjunctive regular path queries. Datalog is sufficient to express most or all of the queries handled in graph databases.

Our code generation framework will be extended to generate specialized code for some recognizable patterns (such as the two-hop optimization explored in this paper) and "canned" best-known algorithms for some specific queries. While a conventional DBMS can be extended similarly, a code generation approach suggests richer opportunities for incorporating user code into optimizations and for library-writing level users to write generators for special classes of queries, as Rompf et al. [25] demonstrated for domain specific languages.

7 Conclusions

We wish to show that relational query languages are an attractive option for modern graph queries on complex data. Our experiments demonstrate that generated C++ code and analogous Grappa code can outperform traditional DBMSs and parallel DBMSs for non-recursive graph queries. Query execution code for Grappa is simple, being symmetric in structure to sequential C++. This simplicity, combined with Grappa's good scalability, makes our code generation an easy and efficient method for relational queries on real-world graphs in a distributed setting.

References

1. neo4j open source graph database, May 2013. http://neo4j.org/
2. Ahmad, Y., Koch, C.: DBToaster: a SQL compiler for high-performance delta processing in main-memory databases. Proc. VLDB Endow. **2**(2), 1566–1569 (2009)
3. Angles, R., Gutierrez, C.: The expressive power of SPARQL. In: Sheth, A.P., Staab, S., Dean, M., Paolucci, M., Maynard, D., Finin, T., Thirunarayan, K. (eds.) ISWC 2008. LNCS, vol. 5318, pp. 114–129. Springer, Heidelberg (2008)
4. Backstrom, L., et al.: Group formation in large social networks: membership, growth, and evolution. In: ACM KDD, pp. 44–54 (2006)
5. Blumofe, R.D., Joerg, C.F., Kuszmaul, B.C., Leiserson, C.E., Randall, K.H., Zhou, Y.: Cilk: An efficient multithreaded runtime system. In: Proceedings of the Fifth ACM SIGPLAN Symposium on Principles and Practice of Parallel Programming, PPOPP 1995, pp. 207–216. ACM, New York (1995)
6. Caverlee, J., Liu, L.: Countering web spam with credibility-based link analysis. In: ACM Principles of Distributed Computing (PODC), pp. 157–166 (2007)
7. Chen, S., Ailamaki, A., Gibbons, P., Mowry, T.: Improving hash join performance through prefetching. In: International Conference on Data Engineering (ICDE), pp. 116–127 (2004)
8. Erling, O., Mikhailov, I.: Virtuoso: RDF support in a native RDBMS. In: de Virgilio, R., Giunchiglia, F., Tanca, L. (eds.) Semantic Web Information Management, pp. 501–519. Springer, Heidelberg (2010)

9. Gonzalez, J.E., et al.: PowerGraph: distributed graph-parallel computation on natural graphs. In: USENIX Operating Systems Design and Implementation (OSDI), pp. 17–30 (2012)
10. Hagberg, A.A., et al.: Exploring network structure, dynamics, and function using NetworkX. In: Python in Science Conference (SciPy), pp. 11–15, August 2008
11. HP-Vertica. Vertica analytics platform, June 2013. http://www.vertica.com
12. Kolda, T.G., Pinar, A., Plantenga, T., Seshadhri, C., Task, C.: Counting triangles in massive graphs with MapReduce. arXiv preprint arXiv:1301.5887 (2013)
13. Kwak, H., Lee, C., Park, H., Moon, S.: What is Twitter, a social network or a news media? In: International Conference on World Wide Web (WWW), pp. 591–600 (2010)
14. Leskovec, J., et al.: Community structure in large networks: natural cluster sizes and the absence of large well-defined clusters. CoRR, abs/0810.1355 (2008)
15. Loo, B.T., et al.: Declarative routing: extensible routing with declarative queries. SIGCOMM Comput. Commun. Rev. 35(4), 289–300 (2005)
16. Losemann, K., Martens, W.: The complexity of evaluating path expressions in SPARQL. In: Proceedings of Principles of Database Systems (PODS) (2012)
17. Malewicz, G., et al.: Pregel: a system for large-scale graph processing. In: ACM SIGMOD, pp. 135–146 (2010)
18. Mandal, A., Fowler, R., Porterfield, A.: Modeling memory concurrency for multi-socket multi-core systems. In: Performance Analysis of Systems Software (ISPASS), March 2010
19. Nelson, J., et al.: Crunching large graphs with commodity processors. In: USENIX Conference on Hot Topics in Parallelism (HotPar), pp. 10–10 (2011)
20. Neumann, T.: Efficiently compiling efficient query plans for modern hardware. Proc. VLDB Endow. 4(9), 539–550 (2011)
21. Neumann, T., Weikum, G.: x-RDF-3X: fast querying, high update rates, and consistency for RDF databases. In: Proceedings of the 36th International Conference on Very Large Data Bases, PVLDB 2013 (2010)
22. Pavan, A., Tangwongan, K., Tirthapura, S.: Parallel and distributed triangle counting on graph streams. Technical report, IBM (2013)
23. Pérez, J., Arenas, M., Gutierrez, C.: Semantics and complexity of SPARQL. In: Cruz, I., Decker, S., Allemang, D., Preist, C., Schwabe, D., Mika, P., Uschold, M., Aroyo, L.M. (eds.) ISWC 2006. LNCS, vol. 4273, pp. 30–43. Springer, Heidelberg (2006)
24. Przyjaciel-Zablocki, M., Schätzle, A., Hornung, T., Lausen, G.: RDFPath: path query processing on large RDF graphs with MapReduce. In: García-Castro, R., Fensel, D., Antoniou, G. (eds.) ESWC 2011. LNCS, vol. 7117, pp. 50–64. Springer, Heidelberg (2012)
25. Rompf, T., Odersky, M.: Lightweight modular staging: a pragmatic approach to runtime code generation and compiled dsls. SIGPLAN Not. 46(2), 127–136 (2010)
26. Seo, J., Guo, S., Lam, M.S.: SociaLite: datalog extensions for efficient social network analysis. In: 29th IEEE International Conference on Data Engineering. IEEE (2013)
27. Waas, F.M.: Beyond conventional data warehousing-massively parallel data processing with Greenplum database. In: Castellanos, M., Dayal, U., Sellis, T. (eds.) BIRTE 2008. LNBIP, vol. 27, pp. 89–96. Springer, Heidelberg (2009)
28. Welc, A., Raman, R., Wu, Z., Hong, S., Chafi, H., Banerjee, J.: Graph analysis: do we have to reinvent the wheel? In: First International Workshop on Graph Data Management Experiences and Systems, GRADES 2013, pp. 7:1–7:6. ACM, New York (2013)

29. Yang, J., Leskovec, J.: Defining and evaluating network communities based on ground-truth. In: ACM SIGKDD Workshop on Mining Data Semantics, pp. 3:1–3:8 (2012)
30. Zhang, W., Zhao, D., Wang, X.: Agglomerative clustering via maximum incremental path integral. Pattern Recogn. **46**, 3056–3065 (2013)

Bringing Linear Algebra Objects to Life in a Column-Oriented In-Memory Database

David Kernert[1,2(✉)], Frank Köhler[2], and Wolfgang Lehner[1]

[1] Database Technology Group, Technische Universität Dresden, Dresden, Germany
wolfgang.lehner@tu-dresden.de
[2] SAP AG, Dietmar-Hopp-Alle 16, Walldorf, Germany
{david.kernert,frank.koehler}@sap.com

Abstract. Large numeric matrices and multidimensional data arrays appear in many science domains, as well as in applications of financial and business warehousing. Common applications include eigenvalue determination of large matrices, which decompose into a set of linear algebra operations. With the rise of in-memory databases it is now feasible to execute these complex analytical queries directly in a relational database system without the need of transfering data out of the system and being restricted by hard disc latencies for random accesses. In this paper, we present a way to integrate linear algebra operations and large matrices as first class citizens into an in-memory database following a two-layered architectural model. The architecture consists of a logical component receiving manipulation statements and linear algebra expressions, and of a physical layer, which autonomously administrates multiple matrix storage representations. A cost-based hybrid storage representation is presented and an experimental implementation is evaluated for matrix-vector multiplications.

1 Introduction

Within the recent decades, data scientists of all domains are increasingly faced with a growing data volume produced by historical events, experiments, and simulations. The era of data deluge and big data has shown the limitation of existing, often non-scalable and domain-specific persistence and computation solutions, which brought scalable database systems back into the discussion. Large numeric data, arranged in vectors and matrices, appear in many science domains, as well as in business warehouse environments. Examples can be found in theoretical nuclear science, genetics, engineering and economical correlation analysis. Analytical algorithms in those fields are often composed of linear algebra operations, including matrix-matrix, matrix-vector and elementwise multiplications. Moreover, linear algebra operations form the building blocks of machine learning algorithms [1] used in data warehousing environments, which is a common domain for commercial databases.

As conventional database management systems (DBMS) neither provide appropriate data objects nor an interface for linear algebra primitives, data scientists rely on custom, highly specialized and hand-written solutions instead.

© Springer International Publishing Switzerland 2015
A. Jagatheesan et al. (Eds.): IMDM 2013/2014, LNCS 8921, pp. 44–55, 2015.
DOI: 10.1007/978-3-319-13960-9_4

However, rather than being responsible for reliable and hardware-dependent solutions, many scientists would prefer to get rid of implementational details. A DBMS with integrated scalable linear algebra implementations could serve as framework that provides basic primitives for their analytical queries, and avoids redundant data copying into any external algebra system. The drop in RAM prices over the last years laid the foundation for shifting databases from hard disc into memory, and analytical queries gained a considerable performance boost on large data sets [2]. By accessing data directly in memory, this development permits to bridge the gap between databases and complex analytical algorithms. Hence, database-integrated linear algebra primitives can now be provided without significant loss of performance, and use cases from the science and business world benefit from such an architecture in many ways:

- **Single source of truth.** The data is persisted and kept consistently in the database, so there is no redundant copying from other data sources to external libraries needed. Furthermore, the corresponding metadata of data sets can be updated synchronously and consistently with the numerical data.
- **Efficient implementation.** Algorithms for linear algebra operations have been researched thoroughly for decades, so there is no need to re-invent the wheel. But tuned linear algebra libraries can be exploited as kernels in the database engine to offer a computational performance that is competitive with existing numeric libraries.
- **Transparency.** A DBMS with our architecture handles different physical storage representations autonomously and provides internally well-partitioned matrices and vectors as self-contained data objects transparent to the user.
- **Manipulation of data.** In common analytic workflows, large matrices are no static objects. As they are manipulated in an iterative process, the data manipulation capabilities of a database will meet the analytical demands better than the tedious maintaining of multiple data files.

This work presents an architectural model for integrating large linear algebra objects and basic operations into a column-oriented in-memory database system. Section 2 provides an overview of recent research about the integration of array structures into databases and efficient linear algebra algorithms in general. The two-layered architectural model, a list of conceptual requirements for the logical data model and its physical mapping to the column store are presented in Sect. 3. Section 4 proposes a hybrid storage representation for large matrices and a strategy to cluster a large matrix into dense and sparse subparts. Our experimental setup and an evaluation of a sparse matrix vector multiplication are shown in Sect. 5. Finally, Sect. 6 summarizes our findings.

2 Related Work

2.1 Linear Algebra in Databases

The gap between the requirements of scientific computing and what is provided by relational databases is a well-known topic in the database community.

Ways to integrate multidimensional array data into the database context have recently been presented by the SciDB [3] team with ArrayQL[1], following the SQL extension SciQL [4]. The latter provides operators for spatial filters used for image processing but it lacks support for linear algebra objects as first class citizens.

A lot of research has been done in the context of data analytics and business intelligence, where linear algebra operations are the building blocks of data mining algorithms. Prior work [5] has shown how vanilla SQL can be used to calculate linear algebra expressions, although they add some user defined functions and infix operators to make the query look more natural. However, they admit that SQL terms rather pair up scalar values than treating vectors as "whole-objects" and does thus not fit the natural way of thinking of a data scientist with a mathematical background. They also state that expressions based on SQL require the knowledge of a certain storage representation, for instance the triple representation for matrices, which is not optimal for many use cases. From a performance perspective, Stonebraker et al. [6] propose the reuse of carefully optimized external C++ libraries as user defined functions for linear algebra calculations, but they leave the problem with resource management and suitable data structures in this "hybrid" world yet unsolved. Another approach based on Hadoop is SystemML [1], where basic linear algebra primitives are addressable via a subset of the R language with a MapReduce backend. Few commercial data warehouse vendors already offer minor support for linear algebra operations integrated in the database engine, but to the best of our knowledge there is no solution which integrates transparent optimization based on topological features of the matrix (e.g., sparsity).

2.2   BLAS and Matrix Multiplications

As we want to provide a solution that is able to compete with hand-tuned implementations, we have to glimpse outside the database world, where efficient linear algebra computation has been thoroughly researched for several decades. It is commonly agreed that a tuned BLAS[2] implementation is the best choice for computing small, dense matrices. Its interface is implemented by specially tuned libraries utilizing single-instruction multiple-data (SIMD) instructions. Libraries are provided by the open-source world or directly by hardware vendors, like ATLAS[3] or Intel MKL[4]. Although the current theoretical lower complexity bound for dense matrix multiplication is $O(n^{2.3727})$, initially presented by Coppersmith and Winograd [7,8], BLAS implementations still rely on the naive $O(n^3)$ algorithm, since the constant of the Coppersmith-Winograd algorithm is simply too high for being practicable. Nevertheless, for very large matrices a recent paper [9] shows that Strassen's Algorithm with the complexity of

---

[1] Array Query Language, http://www.xldb.org/arrayql/.

[2] Basic Linear Algebra Subprograms, http://www.netlib.org/blas/.

[3] Automatically Tuned Linear Algebra Software, http://math-atlas.sourceforge.net/.

[4] Intel Math Kernel Library 11.0, http://software.intel.com/en-us/intel-mkl.

$O(n^{2.8074})$ combined with a NUMA-aware hierarchical storage format outperforms the ATLAS library.

Research on sparse matrices has been less established as for dense, so there were some efforts within the last years to reduce the complexity for fast sparse matrix multiplication from a theoretical perspective [10,11]. Their general idea is to separate the matrix column/row-wise into a dense and a sparse part where the split point is determined by minimizing the number of total algebraic operations, while they admit that their work is only of theoretical value because they rely on Coppersmith-Winograd complexity for rectangular matrix multiplication. This at least confirms our conceptual model to cluster the matrix parts according to their density and treat sparse and dense parts differently. From an algorithmical perspective, there has been recent work on parallel sparse matrix-matrix multiplication [12] and cache-oblivious sparse matrix-vector multiplications [13] using a hypergraph partitioning method.

2.3   Storage Representation of Sparse Matrices

It is widely known that there are various ways to store a sparse matrix, and each of them might be best for a certain situation. The efficiency of a certain storage representation strongly depends on the specific topology of the matrix, since there are typically recurring shapes, such as diagonal, block diagonal or blocked matrices. A comprehensive overview over the different types of sparse storage representation is given in the work of Saad et al. [14]. Storing matrices in hybrid sparse-dense representations, in the way we will present in the remainder of this paper, has – to the best of our knowledge – not been presented in literature so far.

3   Architecture and Requirements

Our architectural model of the linear algebra database engine, sketched in Fig. 1, can be logically separated into two main components: First, the logical layer contains the data model and provides methods to parse linear algebra expressions and choose an appropriate algorithm for the operations to execute. Second, in the physical layer, the storage agent maps the logical linear algebra objects (i.e. matrices and vectors) into the column-oriented storage model by utilizing different internal representations depending on sparsity and shape. The requirements for the *logical* component include:

- **Linear Algebra Query Language.** The common query language of relational databases is SQL, which was originally designed and established for expressions of the relational algebra. As a matter of fact, SQL does not comprise operations or data types of the linear algebra. In order to provide a natural interface for a database user with mathematical background it is crucial to provide matrices, vectors and multidimensional arrays in general as first class citizens. Moreover, for being able to optimize on the logical level, it is also necessary to pass a complete expression string containing basic linear algebra operators to the DBMS.

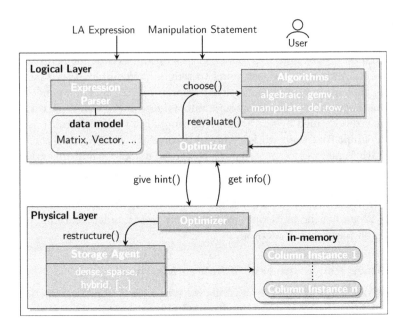

Fig. 1. Linear algebra engine architecture

- **Manipulation Language.** In contrast to a broad perception, matrices in analytical workflows are often *dynamic* objects that underly steady manipulations (e.g., in [15] several base states, which correspond to rows in the Hamiltonean matrix, are truncated before the eigenvalue calculation is repeated). Typical operations on matrices involve insertions, removals, and updates of single elements or whole rows or columns. Such in-place modifications are common in typical database applications, but infeasible with existing linear algebra libraries. The language should therefore offer a way to manipulate linear algebra objects element-, row-, column- and blockwise.
- **Linear Algebra Expression Optimization.** A linear algebra expression consists of operations on an arbitrary number of matrices or vectors. Optimizing the execution order on this layer can help to reduce the number of floating point operations significantly. As an example, consider a multiplication of three matrices $A \in \mathbb{R}^{m \times k}$, $B \in \mathbb{R}^{k \times l}$, $A \in \mathbb{R}^{l \times n}$

$$\text{expression} = \text{``}A \cdot B \cdot C\text{''} \tag{1}$$

Following associations law expression (1) can be evaluated in two ways, either multiply $(A \cdot B)$ first and then C from the right side or multiply $(B \cdot C)$ first and A from the left side. Assuming dense algebra, it turns out that with $k \gg \{l, m, n\}$, the second execution order requires $\frac{2}{1+\epsilon}$ times the number of floating point operations than the first order.

It is noteworthy that this holds only for dense operations, i.e., every matrix element is taken into account, regardless whether it is zero or not. Since multiplications with zero are as expensive as non-zero multiplications, the optimizer should be aware of the sparsity, which might change the optimal execution order. The number of operations N_{op} then can be obtained by considering matrix elements as triple *relations* $\{$row, col, $(A)_{ij}\}$. It is proportional to the join product of two matrix relations A and B with the condition A.col $= B$.row. The multiplication then rather turns into a relational join followed by a projection [10] where techniques of join size estimation (e.g., based on hashing [16]) can be applied to estimate the cost of the sparse algorithm.

Because of the importance of sparsity for optimizing the expression execution, it is desirable that the logical layer receives information about the physical data structure. This should be managed by a globally acting optimizer, which forms the interface between both layers. It combines the physical structure information with statistical information about prevalent algorithmic patterns performed on certain objects, as an efficient execution strongly depends on the conformance between the algorithm and the data representation. This information can in return be passed as a hint to the physical component, which should be able to reorganize the storage representation. The requirements of the *physical* layer are:

- **Multiple In-Memory Storage Representations.** In order to minimize the storage consumption of a large matrix, dense and sparse subparts are stored in separate representations. Each of the storage classes internally uses the native column-oriented storage of the database. As matrices are two-dimensional objects, they cannot be stored naturally in the sequentially addressable columns. Thus, matrices have to be linearized, which is effectively a mapping of matrix elements from the two-dimensional into the one-dimensional space. This is accomplished by ordering the elements according to a certain order (i.e., a space filling curve). 2D-arrays in common programming languages are arranged according to *row-major* (C++, Python) or *column-major* (Fortran, MATLAB) order. Examples for isotropic curves are the *z-curve* (or Morten-order) [17] and the *Hilbert-curve*. The adequacy of the order may depend on specific algorithmic patterns on the object, and as the columns are completely held in memory, the jumps caused by an inappropriate order will at most result in cache misses. However, most numeric libraries require a certain order, and to use them as kernels, our architecture provides a flexible transformation mechanism.
- **Leveraging Parallelization and SIMD Instructions.** In the context of distributed memory there has been recent work about parallel (sparse) matrix-vector and matrix-matrix multiplications [12]. The fundamental trade-off is communication costs versus computation costs, depending on the level of parallelization.

  Low-level parallelization and multithreading is already provided by many numeric libraries, such as ATLAS or Intel MKL. Moreover, most linear algebra calculations degenerate to numerical operations on vectors, thus they fully benefit from SIMD instruction sets. Wherever possible, we want to make use of vendor-provided C++ BLAS kernels that have already been well tuned for the specific hardware characteristics.

- **Data Load.** The common storage format of large scientific data sets that are produced by simulations and experiments are files. Our model foresees an *initial* loading of data from files by using any CSV-parser that connects via a client driver to the database.

4 Topology-Aware Restructuring Using Clustering Strategies

Matrices that are initially loaded into the database are first staged in a temporary sparse structure, for instance in the triple representation. As a consequence, algorithms on staged matrices will in general perform miserably, especially if the matrix has a rather dense topology. The database user does generally not know the topology of the matrix, at least it should not be required to specify the structure in advance. In our model the linear algebra engine restructures the staged matrices by clustering subparts into dense and sparse regions. A reasonable approach is to cluster regions density-based [18], hence classify clusters where the density distribution exceeds a certain threshold as dense and the remaining parts as sparse. The resulting clusters should have rectangular shapes with a minimal extent that should be defined according to the hardware specifications, for example a block should just be large enough to fit into the CPU cache. Figure 2 shows a 800×800 sparse Hamiltonean matrix[5] as an example from nuclear physics research (see Sect. 5.3). For the illustration we used square blocks of dimensions 100×100 and a density-based clustering with the kernel:

$$\mathcal{K}(i, j, i_0, j_0) = \begin{cases} \frac{1}{C} & \text{for } (i, j) \in \text{Block}(i_0, j_0) \\ 0 & \text{else} \end{cases} \tag{2}$$

where i is the row coordinate of a matrix, j the column coordinate, C a normation factor and (i_0, j_0) are the coordinates of a matrix element inside a fixed Block(i_0, j_0). After applying $\mathcal{K}$ to the data of Fig. 2 we effectively get a 2D histogram with 2D block bars of different heights. Figure 3 shows the density distribution relative to two different block density thresholds ρ_c. It can be imagined as a rectangular mountain range in the ocean with a variable water surface level. The higher ρ_c is, the fewer are the remaining dense parts which "protrude" from the surface. The actual question is where to place the cut level ρ_c, which is in general a nontrivial, multidimensional optimization problem.

A $m \times n$ matrix can be clustered into N^C rectangular $m_d^{(j)} \times n_d^{(j)}$ dense regions and $m_{sp}^{(i)} \times n_{sp}^{(i)}$ sparse regions with density ρ_i. Assuming costs τ_{sp} and τ_d for a single element operation in the sparse and dense storage representation,

---

[5] For illustration purposes we regard a relatively small matrix. Depending on the scenario, the matrices can reach dimensions of up to $10^{10} \times 10^{10}$.

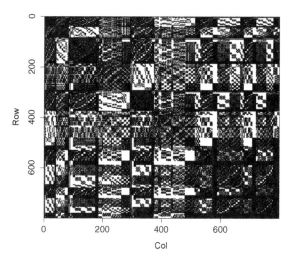

Fig. 2. A 800×800 Hamiltonean matrix resembling the quantum mechanical state of an atomic nucleus in the NCSM model. (Example from theoretical nuclear physics.)

the total cost T of a complete matrix operation[6] on a hybrid representation can be estimated as

$$T = \left(\sum_{j \in \{d\}} A_d \left(m_d^{(j)} n_d^{(j)} \right) \right) \tau_d + \left(\sum_{i \in \{sp\}} A_{sp} \left(N_{nnz}^{(i)} \right) \right) \tau_{sp} + \gamma A_C \left(N^C \right) \quad (3)$$

where $N_{nnz,i} = \rho_i m_{sp}^{(i)} n_{sp}^{(i)}$ is the absolute number of nonzero elements in the ith sparse part. The A's denote the algorithmic complexity of the corresponding algorithm, for instance $A_d(N) = N^{3/2}$ for the naive matrix-matrix multiplication. The last term in (3) refers to the algorithmic overhead, which is connected with the number of subparts N^C. The clustering is ideal if T is minimal. Finding the absolute minimum is generally a nontrivial variational problem in a high-dimensional space. However, depending on the operation, T can degenerate into much simpler expressions, as for the general matrix-vector multiplication (GEMV). The algorithmic access pattern of the GEMV algorithm on a matrix is strictly row-major, thus a row-wise clustering keeps the conformance between algorithm and representation. This effectively means that the m rows of the matrix are clustered into m_{sp} sparse and m_d dense rows. With $A_{d,sp}^{\text{GEMV}}(N) = N$, $n_{d,sp} = n$ and $m_d = m - m_{sp}$ Eq. (3) can be transformed into

$$T^{\text{GEMV}} = nm\tau_d + n \sum_{i}^{m_{sp}} (\rho_i \tau_{sp} - m_{sp} \tau_d) \quad (4)$$

---

[6] T is proportional to the number of single element operations, according to the RAM model.

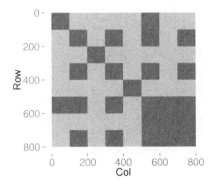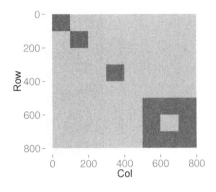

Fig. 3. Matrix density distributions relative to threshold $\rho_c = 0.5$ (left) and $\rho_c = 0.6$ (right). Dark blue denote regions with $\rho_i \geq \rho_c$, light blue means $\rho_i < \rho_c$ (Color figure online).

The right hand side of (4) is minimal if for the *row-density* in the equation $\rho_i < \tau_d/\tau_{sp}$ holds.

5   Experiments and Evaluation

5.1   Experimental Environment

In the context of the column-oriented SAP HANA database, we implemented parts of the physical layer in an in-memory column store prototype. Figure 4 shows the internal mapping of matrices of dense and sparse parts, where $K : \mathbb{N}^n \rightarrow \mathbb{N}$ can generally represent an arbitrary space-filling order (here shown with *row-major* order). Our sparse matrix-vector multiplication algorithm works with pure dense, pure sparse or hybrid representations.

5.2   Evaluation

The platform for our prototype implementation is an Intel Xeon X5650 system with 12 cores and 48 GB RAM. The performance for the GEMV operation was evaluated for sparse matrices in a pure dense, pure sparse and in a hybrid representation, containing subparts according to the density row-based clustering of (4). Without loss of generality, the relative row density was varied using generated matrices following a triangle random distribution to enable a row-based clustering into dense and sparse parts. Moreover we varied the overall density $0.24 < \rho < 1.00$ to illustrate the duality of dense and sparse representations. Figure 5 shows the graph of the measurements for the multiplication of a 12800×12800 matrix with a vector. As expected, the hybrid storage representation is always better than either pure sparse or pure dense. It converges against the performance for sparse matrices for small values of ρ and against the performance for dense matrices for high values of ρ.

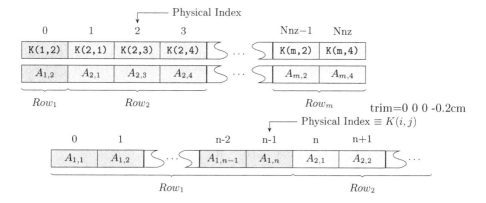

Fig. 4. The upper half shows the sparse representation in two columns: The first column contains the K-coordinate, the second the value of a nonzero element. Below, the dense representation: A single column contains every matrix element, including zero elements.

5.3 Lanczos Algorithm

The Lanczos algorithm is an iterative converging method, similar to the power method, to determine the eigenvalues of a real symmetric matrix. It used to find the energy states of an atomic nucleus, which correspond to the eigenvalues of the quantum mechanical Hamiltonean matrix [15,19]. Technically, the algorithm is composed of iterative sparse matrix-vector multiplications. According to the precision of the model, the Hamiltonean matrix can have arbitrarily many dimensions and can easily consume up to terabytes of storage. In our evaluation we used three matrices of different dimensions. Table 1 shows the speedup

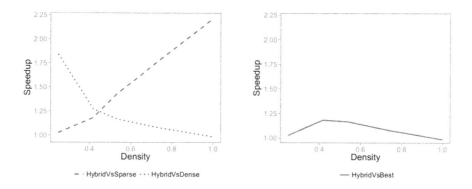

Fig. 5. Speedup in the multiplication of sparse matrices with vectors by using the hybrid representation. On the left side the speedup is shown relative to a pure sparse (dashed line) and pure dense (dotted line), and on the right it is compared to the respective best pure representation.

Table 1. Performance speedup of the multiplication of the sparse Hamiltonean $n \times n$ matrix with a random vector. The evaluation was performed on three matrices of different dimension (i.e. C1A, C2A, C2B) in either pure sparse, pure dense or in the hybrid representation. N^C is the number of subparts. The speedup is shown relative to the pure sparse and to the pure dense representation.

Matrix	n	Nnz	Density	N^C	HybridVsSparse	HybridVsDense
C1A	800	309816	0.484	27	52.0 %	0.1 %
C2A	3440	2930834	0.248	15	3.3 %	39.2 %
C1B	17040	42962108	0.148	60	0.7 %	149.7 %

of the hybrid representation compared to pure dense or pure sparse. There is again a positive speedup for each case, which however becomes less significant for the 17040×17040 matrix. This is substantiated with the complex topology of the matrixes as in Fig. 2, revealing that the rather simple row-based density clustering leaves room for optimization.

6   Summary and Conclusions

The problem of combining linear algebra operations with an efficient and scalable database environment is well-known in the database community as there are various use cases from science and business domains. We showed that it is feasible to integrate complex calculations in in-memory DBMS engines. Our architectural model aimes at applying database principles to linear algebra. It enables dynamic manipulation of matrix data and abstracts the problem of choosing an appropriate algorithm and storage representation from the user by letting the database optimize logical and physical execution. We identified sparsity as the main performance influencing characteristic of large linear algebra objects and proposed hybrid representations mapped to an in-memory column store. A cost-model based density clustering has been proposed to optimize sparse storage structure depending on matrix topology and algorithmic pattern. The evaluation showed that overall performance can benefit from an architecture that combines multiple internal storage representations.

Challenges to our architecture involve the exploitation of efficient BLAS kernels, distribution strategies, and the development of a natural query and manipulation language.

Acknowledgements. We want to thank the group of Prof. Roth from the Institute of Theoretical Nuclear Physics at TU Darmstadt (http://theorie.ikp.physik.tu-darmstadt. de/tnp/index.php) for providing us sparse matrix data and algorithmic insights into their domain-specific problem setting.

References

1. Ghoting, A., Krishnamurthy, R., Pednault, E., Reinwald, B., et al.: SystemML: Declarative machine learning on MapReduce. In: ICDE, pp. 231–242. IEEE (2011)
2. Garcia-Molina, H., Salem, K.: Main memory database systems: an overview. IEEE Trans. Knowl. Data Eng. **4**(6), 509–516 (1992)
3. Brown, P.G.: Overview of SciDB: large scale array storage, processing and analysis. In: SIGMOD, pp. 963–968. ACM (2010)
4. Kersten, M., Zhang, Y., Ivanova, M., Nes, N.: SciQL, a query language for science applications. In: EDBT/ICDT Workshop on Array Databases, pp. 1–12. ACM (2011)
5. Cohen, J., Dolan, B., Dunlap, M., Hellerstein, J.M., et al.: MAD skills: new analysis practices for big data. VLDB **2**(2), 1481–1492 (2009)
6. Stonebraker, M., Madden, S., Dubey, P.: Intel "Big Data" science and technology center vision and execution plan. SIGMOD Rec. **42**(1), 44–49 (2013)
7. Coppersmith, D., Winograd, S.: Matrix multiplication via arithmetic progressions. J. Symb. Comput. **9**(3), 251–280 (1990)
8. Vassilevska Williams, V.: Breaking the coppersmith-winograd barrier (2011)
9. Valsalam, V., Skjellum, A.: A framework for high-performance matrix multiplication based on hierarchical abstractions, algorithms and optimized low-level kernels. CCPE **14**(10), 805–839 (2002)
10. Amossen, R.R., Pagh, R.: Faster join-projects and sparse matrix multiplications. In: ICDT, pp. 121–126. ACM (2009)
11. Yuster, R., Zwick, U.: Fast sparse matrix multiplication. ACM Trans. Algorithms **1**(1), 2–13 (2005)
12. Buluç, A., Gilbert, J.R.: Parallel sparse matrix-matrix multiplication and indexing: implementation and experiments. SIAM J. Sci. Comput. **34**(4), 170–191 (2012)
13. Yzelman, A.N., Bisseling, R.H.: Cache-oblivious sparse matrix-vector multiplication by using sparse matrix partitioning methods. SIAM J. Sci. Comput. **31**(4), 3128–3154 (2009)
14. Saad, Y.: SPARSKIT: A Basic Tool Kit for Sparse Matrix Computations, Version 2 (1994)
15. Roth, R.: Importance truncation for large-scale configuration interaction approaches. Phys. Rev. **C79**, 064324 (2009)
16. Amossen, R.R., Campagna, A., Pagh, R.: Better size estimation for sparse matrix products. In: Serna, M., Shaltiel, R., Jansen, K., Rolim, J. (eds.) APPROX 2010. LNCS, vol. 6302, pp. 406–419. Springer, Heidelberg (2010)
17. Morton, G.: A Computer Oriented Geodetic Data Base and a New Technique in File Sequencing. International Business Machines Company (1966)
18. Hinneburg, A., Keim, D.A.: A general approach to clustering in large databases with noise. Knowl. Inf. Syst. **5**(4), 387–415 (2003)
19. Vary, J.P., Maris, P., Ng, E., Yang, C., Sosonkina, M.: Ab initio nuclear structure the large sparse matrix eigenvalue problem. J. Phys. Conf. Ser. **180**(1), 012083 (2009)

Dynamic Query Prioritization
for In-Memory Databases

Johannes Wust[1]($\boxtimes$), Martin Grund[2], and Hasso Plattner[1]

[1] Hasso Plattner Institute, 14440 Potsdam, Germany
{johannes.wust,hasso.plattner}@hpi.uni-potsdam.de
[2] University of Fribourg, 1700 Fribourg, Switzerland
grund@exascale.info

Abstract. In-memory database management systems have the potential to reduce the execution time of complex operational analytical queries to the order of seconds while executing business transactions in parallel. The main reasons for this increase of performance are massive intra-query parallelism on many-core CPUs and primary data storage in main memory instead of disks or SSDs. However, database management systems in enterprise scenarios typically run a mix of different applications and users, of varying importance, concurrently. As an example, interactive applications have a much higher response-time objective compared to periodic jobs producing daily reports and should be run with priority. In addition to strict prioritization, enforcing a fair share of database resources is desirable, if several users work on applications that share a database. Solutions for resource management based on priorities have been proposed for disk-based database management systems. They typically rely on multiplexing threads on a number of processing units, which is unfavorable for in-memory databases on multi-cores, as single queries are executed in parallel and numerous context switches disrupt cache-conscious algorithms. Consequently, we propose an approach towards resource management based on a task-based query execution that avoids thread multiplexing. The basic idea is to calculate the allowed share of execution time for each user based on the priorities of all users and adjust priorities of tasks of incoming queries to converge to this share.

1 Introduction

In-memory database management systems (IMDBMS) that leverage column-oriented storage have been proposed to run analytical queries directly on the transactional database schema [Pla09]. This enables building analytical capabilities on top of the transactional system, leading to reduced system complexity and reduced overall operating cost. However, running multiple, potentially different applications on a single database instance that records business events leads to a mix of heterogeneous queries that may have different response time objectives.

With TAMEX [WGP13], we have proposed a task-based framework for multiple query class execution on IMDBMS. TAMEX allows to statically prioritize

© Springer International Publishing Switzerland 2015
A. Jagatheesan et al. (Eds.): IMDM 2013/2014, LNCS 8921, pp. 56–68, 2015.
DOI: 10.1007/978-3-319-13960-9_5

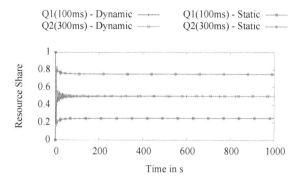

Fig. 1. Comparing static and dynamic query priorities for a single priority class

classes of workloads, for example transactional queries over analytical queries to achieve almost constant response-time of transactions independent of the analytical workload. However, static prioritization falls short on enforcing a fair share of database resources among sessions with different query execution times, since users with similar priorities are scheduled strictly first-in-first-out, independent of the execution time. Enforcing a fair share is desirable in many scenarios, where many users work concurrently on a shared database system.

We further illustrate the shortcoming of static priority-based scheduling using a simple example: Assuming that two concurrent sessions are connected to the database and simultaneously issue queries. As both sessions are connected as analytical clients they will be assigned the same static priority for executing their queries. Now, the first session issues queries that are executed in 100 ms and the second session issues queries against the database that take on average 300 ms. If all queries are executed without think time and sequentially, for simplicity we assume a single processing unit, they will basically interleave. As long as the difference in query execution time between these two sessions is not too big, this will not result in any performance degradations. However, in the above case the average response time of the query will be dominated by the wait latency for the longer query and quickly approach 400 ms. For the heavier query the additional latency does not have as big an impact and it will account for close to 75 % of the consumed resources.

We analyzed this motivating use-case with a scheduling simulator to compare dynamic and static query priorities. Figure 1 shows the result of this simulation. As expected, in the case of the static priorities the second longer query consumes the majority of the resources thus violating the fair- share scheduling. Using dynamic priorities as proposed in detail in this paper, the scheduler will distribute the available resources equally among the two queries independent of the actual run-time of the query.

To summarize the above simulation, we can derive that traditional queue-based scheduling for fair-share scheduling works only well for such scenarios, where the independent time quanta that are executed, are roughly equal or the tasks can be preempted. Both properties do not hold true for task-based scheduling in in-memory databases as tasks can have varying sizes and can be typically not be preempted.

In this paper, we propose an extension of TAMEX that enforces a fair share of database execution time by dynamically adjusting priorities of queries. The remainder of the paper is structured as follows: In the next section, we give a brief overview of the assumed system model and in Sect. 2.2 the task-based query execution with TAMEX. Section 3 describes our model for dynamic query prioritization and Sect. 4 the architecture of our extension to TAMEX. In Sect. 5, we evaluate our proposed solution with an enterprise typical query workload. The next section discusses related work and the last section closes with some concluding remarks and directions for future work.

2 System Model and Task-Based Query Execution

This section gives a brief overview of the underlying system model of an IMDBMS, as well as the task-based query execution framework TAMEX [WGP13], which we use for implementing dynamic query prioritization.

2.1 System Model

We assume an IMDBMS following the system model described in [Pla11], where data is physically stored decomposed in a column-oriented structure. To achieve high read and write performance, an insert-only approach is applied and the data store is split in two parts, a read optimized main partition and a write optimized differential store [KKG+11]. We apply a multi version concurrency control (MVCC) based on transaction IDs (TID) to determine which records are visible to each transaction when multiple transactions run in parallel. See [Pla11] for more details. As our proposed approach for dynamic query prioritization is largely agnostic to specific architectural details of the database. it can be easily generalized and applied to other architecture. However, our approach assumes that the execution of queries can be split in small atomic tasks, which can be executed in parallel, as we will explain in the next section.

2.2 Task-Based Query Execution with TAMEX

This section gives an overview of the task-based query execution framework TAMEX, which is implemented based on HYRISE [GKP+10].

We understand task-based query execution as the transformation of the logical query plan into a set of atomic tasks that represent this plan. These tasks may have data dependencies, but otherwise can be executed independently. We consider such an atomic task as the unit for scheduling. Compared to scheduling whole queries, a task-based approach provides two main advantages: better load balancing on a multiprocessor system, as well as more control over progress of query execution based on priorities. The second advantage is achieved as splitting queries into small units of work introduces natural scheduling intervals during query execution, where lower priority queries can be paused to run higher priority queries without the need of canceling or preempting the low priority query. Assuming a sufficiently small task size, processing units can be freed quickly to execute incoming high priority queries. With the advent of modern many-core processors, the efficient splitting of monolithic queries becomes more and more important as for example stated in [BTAs13].

TAMEX adopts this concept by transforming incoming queries into a directed acyclic graph of tasks and schedules these tasks based on priorities. For TAMEX, we extended HYRISE to support parallel execution of queries, as well as intra-query parallelism, based on multi-threading. Figure 2 provides an overview of the main components of TAMEX and the extensions for dynamic query execution, which are explained later in Sect. 4.2; a more detailed description of TAMEX is provided in [WGP13]. An incoming query is compiled and transformed into a task graph. The task scheduler assigns all ready tasks to a priority queue; all tasks with unmet dependencies are placed into a wait set until they become ready. Worker threads of a threadpool take the tasks from the queue and execute them. Each thread is assigned to a physical processing unit and executes one and only one task. That way, incoming high priority tasks can start immediately executing on all processing units, once the currently running tasks have finished. While this static scheduling approach can effectively prioritize a query class over another, it cannot enforce a fair share of resources if queries with similar priorities are issued. In this paper, we build on TAMEX by setting these priorities dynamically to enforce a given resource share for query classes.

3   Dynamic Shared Query Execution

As motivated in the Introduction, fair resource sharing is of great importance in systems with heterogeneous workloads. In this section, we will introduce the concept of *Dynamic Shared Query Execution* with the goal to approximate a fair resource usage between database sessions on a single system.

In the following, we will describe a new dynamic shared query scheduler with the objective of scheduling queries from independent session on a fair distribution of the available computing hardware. We achieve a good scheduling performance by dynamically re-calculating priorities of the different queries of independent sessions so that resources consumption is better distributed. Since scheduling of queries is a time-critical operation we take special care in optimizing these operations to minimize the impact of dynamically adjusting the priorities. In addition, it is possible to manually decide whether or not dynamic priority adjustments should be made available for the different priority classes. As a result, we maintain high throughput for transactional queries without additional scheduling overhead, but achieve a better flexibility for medium and long running queries.

3.1   Work-Share Definition

We consider a database management system running on a server with N processing units and S open database sessions during an interval T. Each session $s_i \in S$ has an assigned priority p_i and a set of executed queries $Q_i(t)$ at any point in time t during T. Each time a query s finished, it is added to Q_i. We consider online arrival of queries, meaning that the database has no knowledge about the future arrival of queries. Each query $q_{i,j} \in Q_i$ is defined by a set of tasks $O_{i,j}$ and an arrival time $t_{i,j}$. Each task $o_{i,j,n}$ is executed sequentially on one processing unit $n_i \in N$ and has an assigned amount of work $w_{i,j,n}$ processed by the database. In our model, a task has exclusive access to a single processing unit and cannot be preempted.

For each session s_i we determine the work w_i that the database has executed on behalf of this session at a time t, by

$$w_i(t) = \sum_{q_{i,j} \in Q_i(t)} \sum_{o_{i,j,n} \in O_{i,j}} w_{i,j,n} \tag{1}$$

and the total work W processed by the database by

$$W(t) = \sum_{s_i \in S} w_i(t) \tag{2}$$

The share of work ws_i of a session s_i at time t is calculated by

$$ws_i(t) = \frac{w_i(t)}{W(t)} \tag{3}$$

Based on the provided priorities p_i for each session, each query has a target share ts_i, defined by

$$ts_i = \frac{p_i}{\sum_{s_j \in S} p_j} \tag{4}$$

We define the relative share deviation of ws_i from ts_i as

$$\Delta s_i(t) = \frac{ts_i - ws_i(t)}{ts_i} \tag{5}$$

Based on the provided definition, we can formulate the problem of shared query execution as:

Definition 1. Let $S = \{s_1, ..., s_n\}$ be the set of active sessions in an interval T with priorities p_i and queries Q_i, executed on a database with N processing nodes. The problem to solve is to provide an assignment of processing units to tasks $o_{i,j,n}$ during T that minimizes the overall deviation of the work share from the target share over an interval T:

$$\Delta S = \int_0^T \sum_{s_i \in S} |ts_i - ws_i(t)| \tag{6}$$

Due to the online arrival of queries, a scheduling algorithm that assigns process-ing nodes to tasks of queries cannot guarantee optimal schedules. As we assume non-preemptiveness of tasks, it is possible to find examples for which an online algorithm produces results far from optimal [LKA04]. A competitive-analysis or worst-case analysis will produce largely meaningless results. Therefore, we provide a heuristic approach and experimentally validate its effectiveness.

4 Architecture

This section introduces our heuristic approach for approximating the problem described in Sect. 3 and a brief overview of the implementation.

4.1 Approximation of Shared Query Scheduling

The basic idea of our approach is to measure the actual work spent on of query processing for each session and calculate the relative share deviation $\Delta s_i(t)$ for each session $s_i(t)$ between certain points in time t. Based on the ranking of the relative share deviation, we assign priorities to queries with the objective of minimizing the relative share deviation.

To approximate the overall work share deviation for each user, we have imple-mented moving average and exponential smoothing [Bro04], both first and sec-ond order, as heuristics. As we found it hard to justify the choice of parameters for exponential smoothing and as we obtained more predictable results with the moving average, we limit our discussion here on the moving average. To calculate the work shares, we accumulate the work processed for each user, after a task has been completed. In fixed time intervals, we calculate the work share defined in Eq. 3. For the moving average, we take the average work share over the last n intervals to calculate the average work share deviation of Eq. 5:

$$ws_i(t) = \frac{1}{n} \sum_{\{t-n,\ldots,t\}} \frac{w_i(t)}{W(t)} \tag{7}$$

In Eq. 7, $w_i(t)$ defines the accumulated work of session i over the last observed period. To assign the dynamic priorities to the session, we use the work share deviation to sort the sessions and map the priorities accordingly. This approach introduces two parameters that can be modified to adjust the scheduler to the current workload. The first parameter is the window size n of the moving average, as it defines the impact of the currently observed workload compared to the past, and the second parameter is the interval that is used to evaluate a possible change in priorities.

4.2 Architecture for Shared Query Scheduling

We have implemented our approach to approximatively solve the dynamic shared query execution problem described in Sect. 3 based on our database

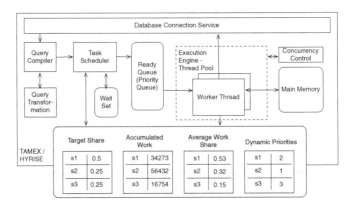

Fig. 2. Dynamic query prioritization based on TAMEX

storage engine HYRISE [GKP+10] and our task-based execution framework
TAMEX [WGP13], introduced in Sect. 2.2.

Figure 2 shows an overview of the extension to TAMEX. For each session,
we keep track of the target share calculated by Eq. 4, the work processed for
each session in the current time interval (indicated as Accumulated Work), the
average work share and the dynamic priorities. After a task is completed, the
execution time of this task is added to the accumulated work for the corresponding session. At the end of an interval, an update process calculates the relative
work share deviation and assigns the dynamic priorities accordingly to minimize
the deviation in the next interval.

The update process consists of the following steps: we calculate the work
share as defined in Eq. 3 by dividing the accumulated work for a session by
the total work of all sessions during the considered interval. Once read, the
accumulated work is reset. Next, we incrementally calculate the average work
share using Eq. 7 and determine the relative work share deviation for each user
using Eq. 5. As a last step, we sort all sessions in descending order by this
deviation and assign dynamic priorities accordingly, giving the highest priority
to the session with the highest relative work share deviation. It is important
to mention, that the worker threads executing tasks are not disrupted by the
update process. Figure 2 illustrates the recorded data and the resulting dynamic
priorities. Session $s3$ gets the highest priority as it has the largest work share
deviation. If the task scheduler places a new task, or one from the *Wait Set* that
becomes ready, in the *ReadyQueue*, it updates the priority of the task according
to the dynamic priority of the session.

To achieve the highest possible accuracy the task scheduler would have to
provide global state information about the actual work of each session that is
then updated by the individual execution threads as soon as a single task is finished. A drawback of this global work share calculation is the global dependency
to accumulate the total work. To alleviate this dependency, we use an atomic
hash-map that maps the individual sessions to a local counter value. Now, this

state is not shared among all execution threads, but only the threads working on tasks of the same session access a unique storage location.

This situation can be additionally improved by keeping a copy of this session map in the thread-local storage of each execution thread that is only lazily collected from the scheduler once it detects a recalculation of the priorities for the tasks. Using the thread-local approach basically avoids contention for the session based work share completely as all manipulations are performed thread-local and only a single consumer will retrieve the individual items.

The adjustment of the dynamic priorities is triggered by the worker threads notifying the task scheduler when a task is finished. If the time interval for calculating an average work share has been passed, the update process, as described above, is initiated. As we need to sort the list of sessions by relative share deviation, the complexity is $O(nlogn)$, with n being the number of sessions. In practice we have compared the performance of TAMEX with and without our extension and could not determine significant performance penalty for up to a 1000 concurrent users.

Since user sessions can be inactive during a period of time when we reevaluate priorities, we only consider those sessions that have issued work over this period of time. As long as the session is inactive, it will not bias the priority calculation; when the session is reactivated, we start the calculation of the moving average again, without considering the share prior to the inactivity.

5   Evaluation

This section provides an experimental evaluation of our approach towards dynamic query prioritization, which we described in Sect. 4. Our test machine is equipped with 2 Intel(R) 5670 CPUs with 6 cores each and 144 GB RAM. The first two experiments demonstrate the effectiveness of our approach to dynamically adjust priorities to converge to a desired target share. In the third experiment, we evaluate parameters for calculating the moving average and derive recommendations for choosing them appropriately.

Motivated by the introductory experiment illustrated in Fig. 1, we have set up an experiment with two sessions, each consisting of a number of equivalent users that issue a stream of queries to the database without think time. Each query consists of two table scans and a join, whereas each operator runs in parallel up to a degree of intra-operator parallelism of 12, corresponding to the number of threads running in parallel. Due to a different size of input tables, the query issued by the users of session 1 (S = 1) takes 40 ms processing time in the database kernel and the query of session 2 (S = 2) 160 ms. Each query has 154 tasks, with a maximum task runtime of about 50 ms for the longer query. We ran the experiment with these two sessions using a round robin scheduler, as well as our fair share scheduler that enforces an equal resource share for both sessions. Each time, the experiment ran for 60 s, whereas the second session started after 10 s and ended after 50 s. We have chosen the window size n of Eq. 7 to be 50 and the interval for updating priorities to 0.2 s.

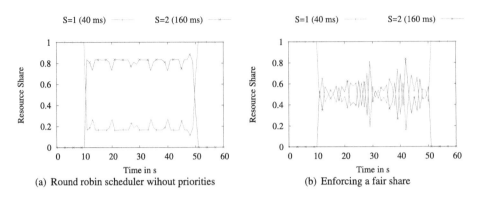

Fig. 3. Two sessions issuing queries with different execution times

Figure 3(a) shows the result for the round robin scheduler. For each second, we have plotted the resource share of the last second. As we take the point of view of a user outside of the database, we count work processed for a session at the point of time when an entire query is finished, as opposed to single tasks. In line with our expectations from the simulation, applying a round robin scheduler leads to a share equal to the ratio of the runtime of both queries. In Fig. 3(b), we see that the dynamic prioritization of queries leads to a varying resource share of each queries averaging to a fair share over the interval between 10 and 50 s. While the round robin fails to distribute the resources equally among the two sessions, it becomes possible to efficiently schedule queries with different runtimes and to distribute the resources equally when applying dynamic query prioritization.

Figure 4 demonstrates the applicability of our approach to a larger number of sessions and different priorities. This time, all sessions S consist of a single user issuing a stream of the query described above with 160ms processing time when executed as a single query on the system. When scheduling all incoming tasks with a round robin scheduler, each query gets approximately the same share of the system resources (Fig. 4(a)). In Fig. 4(b), we assigned User 1 a priority of 4 ($P = 4$) and the remaining users a priority of 1 ($P = 1$) with the objective of enforcing a share of 50 % of the total resources for User 1 and 12.5 % for each of the other users during the interval when all users issue queries in parallel. In this experiment, our dynamic query prioritization is able to schedule the queries of all the different sessions according to the assigned priorities.

Choosing the window size for the moving average and the interval length of updating priories is a trade-off between overall accuracy and adaptation time to react on changes in the workload. To illustrate this, we have tested five sessions with equal priorities, issuing a constant stream of queries. One session issues a query with 160 ms runtime, the other users a query with 40 ms run time. We start all users at the same time and measure the cumulated work share since the start for 60 s. Figure 5 shows the results for the calculation of the relative share deviation with moving average for different window sizes (w) and interval lengths (i) for one of the five sessions with query length 160 ms.

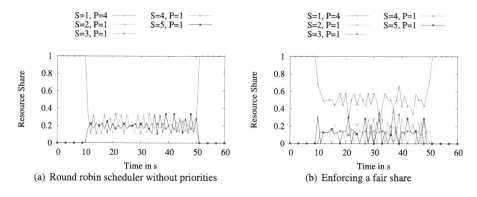

Fig. 4. Five sessions issuing queries (160 ms) with different priorities

In Fig. 5(a), we have changed the window size for the moving average and kept the size of the observation interval constant at 1s. As expected, a larger window size leads to a smoother curve that converges to the target share of 20 % without major deviations. A smaller window size shows more spikes, as intervals with above or below average have a larger impact on calculated work share, but also adapts faster to workload changes. However, if the window size is chosen too small, as it is here the case for size 5, the scheduler cannot enforce the overall target share anymore, as the sample size is too small.

In Fig. 5(b), we changed the interval lengths for the moving average and kept the window size constantly at 20. For small interval lengths of 0.1 s, the total time interval of window size multiplied with interval lengths that is considered becomes so small, that the scheduler cannot systematically decrease the performance of the user with the long running query to enforce the target share. The share of this user is closer now to the share of the round robin scheduler. A large

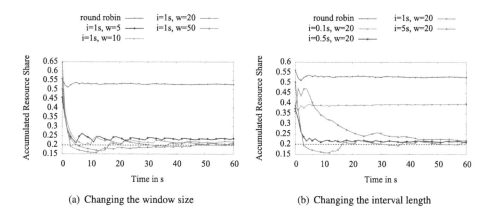

Fig. 5. Comparing parameters for calculating work share deviation with moving average

window size leads to less adjustments of priority and therefor takes longer to converge, but is more robust to changes in the workload.

Choosing the parameters depends on the number of concurrent connections and task sizes and is thus workload dependent. To adapt to changing workloads the scheduler has to observe these parameters and adjust accordingly. The goal for the scheduler is then to chose the interval to be large enough to include a significant number of tasks from each active session, allowing to determine a trend of the work share applying the current set of priorities. It is important to mention, that it does not dependent on the entire runtime of the issued queries. The window size has to be chosen based on the average number of tasks a session executes per interval and the average execution time per task. For shorter sessions, e.g. occurring in interactive applications, a smaller window size helps to quickly balance the load and avoid that one session gets too many resources.

6 Related Work

Workload management for heterogeneous queries has been frequently in the context of web requests [BSUK07, MSAHb03, SHBI+06] and business intelligence applications [BCD+92, KDW+10]. In contrast to our research, most work on workload management was specific to disk-based DBMS and considered a query as the level for scheduling. In general, we can divide the proposed approaches for managing workloads of different query classes into two classes: *external* and *internal*. The general idea of external workload management is to control the number of queries that access the database (admission control). Internal workload management systems typically control available resources, such as CPU or main memory, and assign them to queries. Niu et al. [NMP09] give a more detailed overview of workload management systems for DBMS.

Early work on internal workload management has been published by Carey et al. [BCD+92, CJL89]. The simulation studies are specific to disk-based DBMS, as they extensively model disk-based DBMS characteristics such as disk rotation time or buffer management. A more recent work by McWherter et al. [MSAHb03] shows the effectiveness of scheduling bottleneck resources using priority-based algorithms in a disk-based DBMS. Narayanan et al. [NW11] propose a system for dynamic prioritization of queries to meet given priorities for query classes. In contrast to our work these approaches rely on multiplexing threads on a number of processing units and achieve a targeted resource share either centrally, by prioritizing threads on OS-level or collaboratively, by letting each thread check its consumed resources regularly and sleeping if a certain quota has been met. These strategies are unfavorable for in-memory databases on multi-cores, as execution time is largely dominated by cache locality which is disrupted by context switches.

More recent work has proposed solutions for adaptive admission control based on query response time. Schroeder et al. [SHb06, SHBI+06] propose an external queue management system that schedules queries based on defined service-levels per query-class and a number of allowed queries in the database, the so-called multiprogramming level. Niu et al. [NMP09] propose a solution that manages a mixed workload of OLTP and OLAP queries by controlling the resources assigned to OLAP queries depending on the response times of OLTP queries. Krompass et al. [KKW+10] extended this approach for multiple objectives. The work of Kuno et al. [KDW+10] and Gupta et al. [GMWD09] propose mixed workload schedulers with admission control based on query run-time prediction. Although external workload management systems are applicable to in-memory databases, they fall short in our scenario, as queries need to get access to a large number of processing units quickly, e.g. to answer complex interactive queries.

Until recently, scheduling in operating systems and query scheduling in database management systems were working very differently since queries in DBMS cannot be as easily preempted and were typically very monolithic. With modern many-core systems, task-based decomposition gives the scheduler in DBMS more flexibility and we are able to adapt concepts like [XWY+12] to allow fair scheduling of tasks in IMDBMS.

7   Conclusion and Future Work

In this paper, we have shown that a dynamic priority-based query scheduling can be effectively applied for IMDBMS to fairly schedule mixed enterprise workloads. We are planning to further evaluate the performance of our scheduling approach and extend TAMEX to leverage further information about task characteristics in scheduling decisions. We are further planning to take resource requirements besides CPU, such as cache and memory bandwidth into account to place tasks in a way that will minimize resource conflicts.

References

[BCD+92] Brown, K., Carey, M., DeWitt, D., Mehta, M., Naughton, F.: Resource allocation and scheduling for mixed database workloads, Jan 1992. http://www.cs.wisc.edu

[Bro04] Brown, R.G.: Smoothing, Forecasting and Prediction of Discrete Time Series (Dover Phoenix editions). Dover Publications, New York (2004)

[BSUK07] Biersack, E.W., Schroeder, B., Urvoy-Keller, G.: Scheduling in practice. SIGMETRICS Perform. Eval. Rev. **34**(4), 21–28 (2007)

[BTAs13] Balkesen, C., Teubner, J., Alonso, G., Tamer szu, M.: Main-memory hash joins on multi-core CPUs: tuning to the underlying hardware. In: IEEE Computer Society ICDE '13 (2013)

[CJL89] Carey, M.J., Jauhari, R., Livny, M.: Priority in DBMS resource scheduling. In: VLDB, pp. 397–410 (1989)

[GKP+10] Grund, M., Krüger, J., Plattner, H., Zeier, A., Cudre-Mauroux, P., Madden, S.: HYRISE: a main memory hybrid storage engine. Proc. VLDB Endow. **4**(2), 105–116 (2010)

[GMWD09] Gupta, C., Mehta, A., Wang, S., Dayal, U.: Fair, effective, efficient and differentiated scheduling in an enterprise data warehouse. In: EDBT '09, pp. 696–707. ACM, New York, NY, USA (2009)

[KDW+10] Kuno, H., Dayal, U., Wiener, J.L., Wilkinson, K., Ganapathi, A., Krompass, S.: Managing dynamic mixed workloads for operational business intelligence. In: Kikuchi, S., Sachdeva, S., Bhalla, S. (eds.) DNIS 2010. LNCS, vol. 5999, pp. 11–26. Springer, Heidelberg (2010)

[KKG+11] Krueger, J., Kim, C., Grund, M., Satish, N., Schwalb, D., Chhugani, J., Dubey, P., Plattner, H., Zeier, A.: Fast updates on read-optimized databases using multi-core CPUs. PVLDB $5(1)$, 61–72 (2011)

[KKW+10] Krompass, S., Kuno, H., Wilkinson, K., Dayal, U., Kemper, A.: Adaptive query scheduling for mixed database workloads with multiple objectives. In: DBTest '10, pp. 1:1–1:6. ACM, New York, NY, USA (2010)

[LKA04] Leung, J., Kelly, L., Anderson, J.H.: Handbook of Scheduling: Algorithms, Models, and Performance Analysis. CRC Press Inc, Boca Raton, FL, USA (2004)

[MSAHb03] Mcwherter, D.T., Schroeder, B., Ailamaki, A., Harchol-balter, M.: Priority mechanisms for OLTP and transactional web applications, pp. 535–546 (2003)

[NMP09] Niu, B., Martin, P., Powley, W.: Towards autonomic workload management in DBMSs. J. Database Manage. $20(3)$, 1–17 (2009)

[NW11] Narayanan. S., Waas, F.: Dynamic prioritization of database queries. In: IEEE Computer Society ICDE '11, Washington, DC, USA (2011)

[Pla09] Plattner, H.: A common database approach for OLTP and OLAP using an in-memory column database. In: SIGMOD, pp. 1–2 (2009)

[Pla11] Plattner, H.: SanssouciDB: an in-memory database for processing enterprise workloads. In: BTW, pp. 2–21 (2011)

[SHb06] Schroeder, B., Harchol-balter, M.:. Achieving class-based QoS for transactional workloads. In: Proceedings of the IEEE ICDE, p. 153 (2006)

[SHBI+06] Schroeder, B., Harchol-Balter, M., Arun, I., Nahum, E., Wierman, A.: How to determine a good multi-programming level for external scheduling. In: International Conference on Data Engineering vol. 60 (2006)

[WGP13] Wust, J, Grund, M., Plattner, H.: TAMEX: a task-based query execution framework for mixed enterprise workloads on in-memory databases. INFORMATIK, Koblenz (accepted for publication). In: Workshop on In-Memory Data Management (2013)

[XWY+12] Xu, D., Wu, C., Yew, P.C., Li, J., Wang, Z.: Providing fairness on shared-memory multiprocessors via process scheduling. In:ACM SIG-METRICS/PERFORMANCE, SIGMETRICS '12, pp. 295–306. ACM, New York, NY, USA (2012)

Aggregates Caching in Columnar In-Memory Databases

Stephan Müller[⊠] and Hasso Plattner

Hasso Plattner Institute, University of Potsdam, Potsdam, Germany
{stephan.mueller,hasso.plattner}@hpi.uni-potsdam.de

Abstract. The mixed database workloads found in enterprise applications are comprised of short-running transactional as well as analytical queries with resource-intensive data aggregations. In this context, caching the query results of long-running queries is desirable as it increases the overall performance. However, traditional caching approaches are inefficient in a way that changes in the base data result in invalidation or recalculation of cached results.

Columnar in-memory databases with a main-delta architecture are well-suited for a novel caching mechanism for aggregate queries that is the main contribution of this paper. With the separation into read-optimized main storage and write-optimized delta storage, we do not invalidate cached query results when new data is inserted to the delta storage. Instead, we use the cached query result and combine it with the newly added records in the delta storage. We evaluate this caching mechanism with mixed database workloads and show how it compares to existing work in this area.

1 Introduction

The classic distinction between online transactional processing (OLTP) and online analytical processing (OLAP) is no longer applicable in the context of modern enterprise applications [1,2]. Instead of associating transactional or analytical queries with separate applications, a single modern enterprise application executes both – transactional *and* analytical – queries. Within the available-to-promise (ATP) application, for example, the OLTP-style queries represent product stock movements whereas the OLAP-style queries aggregate over the product movements to determine the earliest possible delivery date for requested goods by a customer [3]. Similarly, in financial accounting, every financial accounting document is created with OLTP-style queries, while a profit and loss statement needs to aggregate over all relevant documents with OLAP-style queries that are potentially very expensive [1].

To speed-up the execution of long-running queries, techniques such as *query caching* and the introduction of *materialized views* have been proposed [4]. However, the inherent problem with query caching and materialized views is that whenever the base data is modified, these changes have to be propagated to ensure consistency. While a database query cache can simply flush or invalidate the cache, a process known as *materialized view maintenance*, is well established

A. Jagatheesan et al. (Eds.): IMDM 2013/2014, LNCS 8921, pp. 69–81, 2015.
DOI: 10.1007/978-3-319-13960-9_6

in academia [4–6] and industry [7,8] but with focus on traditional database architectures and data warehousing [6,9,10]. For purely analytical applications, a maintenance downtime may be acceptable, but this is not the case in a mixed workload environment as transactional throughput must always be guaranteed. Also, the recent trend towards columnar in-memory databases (IMDBs) that are able to handle transactional as well as analytical workloads on a single system [11–13] has not been considered.

A columnar IMDB for transactional and analytical workloads has some unique features and preferred modes of operating [1,2]. To organize the attributes of a table in columns and to encode the attribute values via a dictionary into integers, known as dictionary encoding [14], has many advantages such as high data compression rates and fast attribute scans. But this organization comes at a certain price. In transactional workloads we have to cope with high insert rates. A permanent reorganization of the attribute vectors (columns) would not allow for a decent transactional performance, because new values appear and have to be included in the encoding process which complicates the request to keep the attribute dictionaries sorted. A way out of this dilemma is to split the attribute vectors of a table into a read-optimized main storage and a write-optimized delta storage. All new inserts, updates, and deletes are appended to the delta storage with separate unsorted dictionaries. At certain times the attribute vectors are merged with the ones in the main storage and a new dictionary (per attribute) is established [15]. Since the main storage is significantly larger than the delta, the insert performance becomes acceptable and the analytic performance is still outstanding [16].

The fact that we can handle transactional and analytical workloads in one system has tremendous benefits to the users of the system. Not only the freedom of choice what and how to aggregate data on demand but the instant availability of analytical responses on even large operational data sets will change how business will be run. A consequence of this desirable development will be a significant increase in the analytical workload with aggregate queries on the combined system.

To cope with the increase of analytical queries on transactional data, we propose an aggregate query caching mechanism that leverages the main-delta architecture of columnar in-memory databases. Because of the separation into main and delta storage, we do not invalidate cached aggregate queries when new records are inserted to the delta storage. Instead, we use the cached results of the aggregate queries in the main storage and combine them with the newly inserted records in the delta storage.

After discussing related work in Sect. 2, we outline the algorithm and architecture of our implementation in Sect. 3. In Sect. 4 we evaluate our caching mechanism and conclude with an outlook on future work in Sect. 5.

2   Related Work

The caching of aggregate queries is closely related to the introduction of materialized views to answer queries more efficiently. To be more precise, a cached query result is a relation itself and can be regarded as a materialized view. Gupta gives a good overview of materialized views and related problems in [4]. Especially, the problem of materialized view maintenance has received significant attention in academia [5,6,17]. Database vendors have also investigated this problem thoroughly [7,8] but to the best of our knowledge, there is no work that evaluates materialized view maintenance strategies in columnar in-memory databases with mixed workloads. Instead, most of the existing research is focused on data warehousing environments [6,9,10] where maintenance downtimes may be acceptable.

The summary-delta tables concept to efficiently update materialized views with aggregates comes close to our approach as the algorithm to recalculate the materialized view is based on the old view and the newly inserted, updated, or deleted values [18]. However, this approach updates the materialized views during a maintenance downtime in a warehousing environment and does not consider the newly inserted operational data during query processing time which is necessary in a transactional environment. Further, it does not take the main-delta architecture and the resulting merge process into account.

3   Aggregates Caching

In this section, we describe the basic architecture of our aggregate query caching mechanism and the involved algorithms. The cache is implemented in a way that is transparent to the application. Consequently, the caching engine has to ensure data consistency by employing an appropriate maintenance strategy.

While aggregate functions can be categorized into distributive, algebraic and holistic functions [19] we limit our implementation to distributive functions without the `distinct` keyword, such as `sum`, `min`, `max`, or `count` as they are most commonly found in analytical queries [16] and because they are self-maintainable with respect to insertions [18]. Updates and deletes require an extension of our algorithm as explained in Sect. 3.5. Since algebraic functions can be computed by combining a constant number of distributive functions, e.g., `avg = sum / count`, they can also be supported given the assumption that a cached aggregate query with an `avg` function is rewritten to include both the `sum` and `count` functions.

3.1   Architecture and Algorithm

The basic architecture of our aggregates caching mechanism is illustrated in Fig. 1. With the columnar IMDB being divided into main and delta storage, the aggregates caching manager component can distinguish between these and read the delta storage explicitly and combine this result with the cached query result. The relations of cached aggregate queries are each stored in a separate database table. Further, a global cache management table (CMT) stores the meta data for each cached aggregate query including access statistics. Also, it maps the hash of the normalized SQL string to the database table that holds the cached results of the aggregate query.

Every parsed query with supported aggregate functions, is handled through the aggregates caching manager. To check if the query already exists in the cache,

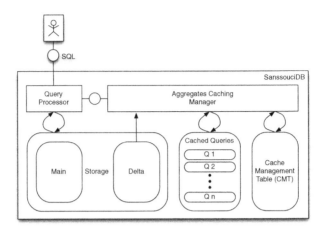

Fig. 1. Aggregates query caching architecture

the hash value of the normalized SQL string is computed and looked up in the CMT. If the aggregates caching manager does not find an existing cache entry for the corresponding SQL query, it conveys the query without any changes to the underlying main and delta storage. After query execution, it is checked whether the query is suitable for being cached depending on the cache admission policy (cf. Sect. 3.6). If this is the case, the query result from the main storage is cached for further reuse. This is done by creating a separate table that only contains the results of the specific query. The name of the table equals the generated hash value of the SQL string and is referenced by the CMT.

Listing 1.1. A simple aggregate query

```
SELECT month, account, SUM(amount) FROM sales
WHERE year=2013 GROUP BY month, account
```

In case, the query is already cached, the original aggregate query (an example is shown in Listing 1.1) is executed on the delta storage. Listing 1.2 shows how the result from the delta storage is combined with the cached query result as persisted in the table **agg08f15e** (assuming that agg08f15e is the hash of the example query sql string) and returned to the query processor. We use a **UNION ALL** query to not eliminate duplicates, but aggregate them by applying the original aggregate query on the combined results.

Listing 1.2. Combining the cached aggregate query with results from the delta storage

```
SELECT month, account, SUM(amount) FROM
    (SELECT * FROM agg08f15e
    UNION ALL
    SELECT month, account, SUM(amount)
    FROM sales_delta
    WHERE year=2013 GROUP BY month, account)
WHERE year=2013 GROUP BY month, account
```

3.2   Aggregates Maintenance Strategies

To ensure consistency, cached aggregate queries have to be maintained accordingly. The timing of existing materialized view maintenance strategies can be distinguished between *eager* and *lazy*. While eager strategies immediately propagate each change of base tables to the affected materialized views [5], lazy (or deferred) strategies maintain materialized views no later than the time the materialized view is queried [8]. Independently of the timing, one can divide maintenance strategies into *full* and *incremental* ones. Full strategies maintain the aggregate by complete recalculation using its base tables. Incremental strategies store recent modifications of base tables and explicitly use them to maintain the views. Based on the fact that an incremental calculation of aggregates is always more efficient than a full recalculation [6], we focus on incremental strategies, despite the fact that some aggregate functions cannot be maintained incrementally [18].

The proposed aggregate query caching mechanism does neither maintain the cached aggregate at insert time nor at query time. Instead, it is done incrementally during the delta merge process. Since it is possible to predict the query execution time of in-memory databases very accurately [20], we create cost models for each maintenance strategy. The costs are based on a simplified workload model that consists of a number of records N_w written into the base table and a number of read aggregates N_r of the cached aggregate queries.

Eager Incremental Update (EIU). Since the cached aggregate query is maintained after each insert, the cost for accessing the aggregate query is just a single read. The maintenance costs are tied to a write into the base table. As it is an incremental strategy, the costs consist of the read time T_{RA} to retrieve the old value and the write time T_W for the new value into the cached aggregate table.

Lazy Incremental Update (LIU). All maintenance is done on the first read accessing the cached aggregate query. The maintenance costs $N_{w_k} \cdot (T_{RA} + T_W)$ and cost to read the requested aggregate T_{RA} are combined into one function. The maintenance costs depend on the number of writes with distinct grouping attribute values per read N_{w_k} which is influenced by the order of the queries in a workload and the distribution of the distinct grouping attributes.

Merge Update (MU). The costs of a read T_{r_k} is the sum of an access to the cached aggregate query T_{RA} and an on-the-fly aggregation on the delta table whereas T_{RD_k} defines the costs for the aggregation for the kth read. The merge update strategy updates its materialized aggregate table during a merge process. Therefore, the tuples in delta storage have to be considered. The merge time T_m for the number of cached aggregates N_A is the sum of a complete read of the cached aggregate query tables $N_A \cdot T_{RA}$, a read of the delta T_{RD_k}, and the write of the new aggregate $(N_A + N_{newWD}) \cdot T_W$. Equation 1 shows the calculation of the total execution time based on the time for reads and the merge.

$$T_{total} = N_m \cdot T_m + N_r \cdot T_{r_k} \tag{1}$$

3.3   Optimal Merge Interval

The costs of our aggregates caching mechanism and the MU maintenance strategy mainly depend on the aggregation performance on the delta storage which decreases linearly with an increasing number of records [21]. However, the merge operation also generates costs that have to be considered. In the following, we propose a cost model which takes the costs for the merge operation and the costs for the aggregation on the delta storage into account. Similarly to the cost model for the merge operation introduced by Krüger et al. [15], our model is based on the number of accessed records to determine the optimal merge interval for one base table of a materialized view.

Equation 2 calculates the number of records $Costs_{total}$ that are accessed during the execution of a given workload. A workload consists of a number of reads N_r and a number of writes N_w. The number of merge operations is represented by N_m. The first summand represents the accesses that occur during the merge operations. Firstly, each merge operation has to access all records of the initial main storage $|C_M|$. Secondly, previously merged records and new delta entries are accessed as well [15]. This number depends on the number of writes N_w in the given workload divided by two (since the number of records in the delta increases linearly). The second summand determines the number of accesses for all reads N_r on the delta. As before, the delta grows linearly and is speed-up by the number of merge operations N_m.

$$Costs_{total} = N_m \cdot (|C_M| + \frac{N_w}{2}) + N_r \cdot \frac{\frac{N_w}{2}}{N_m + 1} \tag{2}$$

$$Costs'_{total} = |C_M| + \frac{N_w}{2} - \frac{N_r \cdot N_w}{2 \cdot N_m^2 + 4 \cdot N_m + 2} \tag{3}$$

$$N_m = \frac{\sqrt{2 \cdot |C_M| \cdot N_w \cdot N_r + N_w^2 \cdot N_r} - 2 \cdot |C_M| - N_w}{2 \cdot |C_M| + N_w} \tag{4}$$

The minimum is calculated by creating the derivation (Eq. 3) of our cost model and by obtaining is root (Eq. 4). N_m represents the number of merge operations. Dividing the total number of queries by N_m returns the optimal merge interval.

3.4   Join Operations

When processing aggregate queries with join operations, the complexity of the caching mechanism and the involved MU maintenance strategy increases. Instead of combining the cached result with the query result on the delta storage, the join of every permutation has to be computed before these results can be combined. In Fig. 2, we have illustrated the involved tables in the main and delta partition of a simple aggregate query including a join of two tables. While the cached query result is based on a join of the header and line_items table in the main partition, we have to compute the joins of header' and line_items' tables in

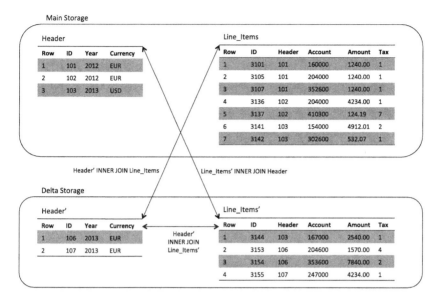

SELECT Header.Year, SUM(Line_Items.Amount) FROM Header INNER JOIN Line_Items GROUP BY Header.Year

Fig. 2. Aggregate queries with join operations

the delta partition, and additionally the joins between `header'` and `line_items` as well as `line_items'` and `header`. When the cached aggregate query consists of three or more joined tables, the necessary join operations between delta and main storage increase exponentially. The number of necessary joins based on the number of tables t in the aggregate query can be derived as $JoinOps = 2^t - 1$.

After analyzing enterprise workloads, we found out that aggregates for accounting, sales, purchasing, stocks etc. always need a join of the transaction header and the corresponding line items. Interestingly, new business objects such as sales orders or accounting documents are always inserted as a whole, therefore the new header and the new line items are persisted in the delta storage. Using these semantics of the business objects can reduce the number of necessary join operations from three to just one (a join of header and line items in the delta). In case a business object can be extended after the initial insert, the header entry could already be merged into the main storage. Consequently, we would need an additional join of the `line_items'` table in the delta with the `header` table in the main.

3.5 Updates and Deletes

The presented algorithm is valid for an insert-only approach which handles logical updates or deletes by inserting differential values to the delta storage. When updating a tuple, and only inserting the new, updated value to the delta storage, the algorithm needs to be extended. We have identified two possible solutions:

We can either retrieve the old value from main storage, calculate the differential value and insert this value in the delta storage and flag it accordingly, so that the merge process does not consider this tuple. Or, to avoid an adaption of the merge process, we could also maintain a separate data structure that holds the differential values for all updates or deletes and include these values in the delta aggregate query.

Min and max functions are not self-maintainable and therefore, for every update or delete, we have to perform additional checks. For deletes, we have to check if the deleted tuple is a min or max tuple. For updates, we have to check if the updated value is higher than a cached max aggregate or lower than a cached min aggregate. If that is the case, the cached min or max aggregate has to be invalidated and recalculated from the main and delta storage.

Despite the inherent overhead, we believe that this process is viable, because the percentage of updates and deletes is very low in enterprise applications [15].

3.6   Cache Management Strategies

In order to limit the needed memory space and reduce the inherent computational overhead of the caching algorithm, we only want to admit the most profitable aggregate queries to the cache. The query cache management takes place at query execution time for cache admission and replacement, and during the merge process to determine which aggregate queries to incrementally maintain or to evict from the cache.

We have identified two approaches to determine whether to cache an aggregate query after it has been executed: The first way is to measure the execution time of the aggregate query and only cache queries that are above a system-defined threshold. Another way is to calculate the profit of using a cached query over an on-the-fly aggregation. The definition of the profit for query Q_i can be described with the execution time for the aggregation on the main storage $AggMain_i$ and delta storage $AggDelta_i$ divided by the time to access a cached aggregate query $AggCached_i$ and the execution time of the aggregation on the delta storage $AggDelta_i$.

$$profit(Q_i) = \frac{AggMain_i + AggDelta_i}{AggCached_i + AggDelta_i} \qquad (5)$$

This profit metric will change when the delta storage grows, but it is a good initial indicator to decide which queries to admit to the cache. When the cache size reaches a system-defined size limit, we can replace queries with lower profits or execution times by incomings queries with higher profits or execution times.

During the merge process, it has to be decided which cached aggregate query to incrementally update or evict from the cache. For this process, we can use another metric that includes the average frequency of execution λ_i of query Q_i which is calculated based on the K_ith last reference and the difference between the current time t and the time of the last reference t_K:

$$\lambda_i = \frac{K_i}{t - t_K} \qquad (6)$$

The profit of a query Q_i can then be extended as follows:

$$profit(Q_i) = \frac{\lambda_i \cdot (AggMain_i + AggDelta_i)}{AggCached_i + AggDelta_i} \tag{7}$$

4 Evaluation

We implemented the concepts of the presented aggregates caching mechanism in SanssouciDB [16] but believe that an implementation in other columnar IMDBs with a main-delta architecture such as SAP HANA [11] or Hyrise [13] will lead to similar results. Instead of relying on a mixed workload benchmark such as the CH-benchmark [22], we chose an enterprise application that generates a mixed workload to the database with real customer data. The identified financial accounting application covers OLTP-style inserts for the creation of accounting documents as well as OLAP-style queries to generate reports such as a profit and loss statement. The inserts were generated based on the original customer data set covering 330 million records in a denormalized single table. We then extracted 1,000 OLAP-style aggregate queries from the application and validated these with domain experts. The query pattern of the aggregate queries contain at least one aggregate function with optional group by clauses and predicates. Further, nested subqueries are supported. Mingling both query types according to the creation times (inserts) and typical execution times (aggregate queries) yielded a mixed workload which our evaluations are based upon.

4.1 Aggregates Caching

The strength of a caching mechanism is to answer recurring queries. To compare our approach to a standard query cache that gets invalidated whenever the base data changes, we have created a benchmark based on a mixed workload of 10,000 queries with 90 % analytical queries and 10 % transactional insert queries. The 9,000 analytical aggregate queries were randomly generated from the 1,000 distinct queries. The average execution time on a 40 core server with 4 Intel Xeon E7-4870 CPU each having 10 physical cores and 1 TB of main memory when using no cache was 591 ms which dropped down to 414 ms with a standard query cache. The average execution time of the aggregates cache was at 74 ms, outperforming the standard query cache by nearly a factor of six.

With an increasing number of distinct aggregate queries, the performance of the proposed aggregates caching mechanisms decreases linearly. With a workload of 100 % distinct aggregate queries, where no cache reuse takes place, we measured the overhead of the aggregates caching mechanism. When caching every incoming aggregate query, this overhead was at 7 % compared to not using the cache, mainly due to the execution time of creating the table that holds the results of the cached aggregate query.

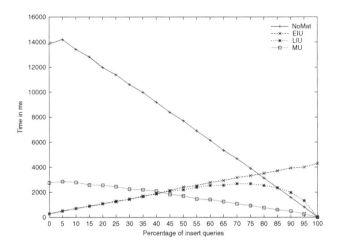

Fig. 3. Measuring the total time of a workload with a varying ratio of inserts.

4.2 Aggregates Maintenance Strategies Under Varying Workloads

To compare the aggregates caching mechanisms and the involved maintenance strategy to the strategies described in Sect. 3.2, we have changed the benchmark to varying read/write ratios and a workload of 1,000 queries. A read represents an analytical query with an aggregation and a write represents an insert to the base table which contains one million records. The results as depicted in Fig. 3 reveal that when using no materialization (NoMat), the time to execute the workload decreases with an increasing ratio of inserts because an on-the-fly aggregation is more expensive than inserting new values. The EIU and LIU strategies use materialized aggregates to answer selects and perform much better with high select ratios than no materialization. EIU and LIU have almost the same execution time for read-intensive (less than 50 % inserts) workloads. Reads do not change the base table and the materialized aggregates stay consistent. Hence, maintenance costs do not dominate the execution time of the workload and the mentioned strategies perform similarly. With an increasing number of inserts, the performance of EIU decreases nearly linearly while LIU can condense multiple inserts within a single maintenance step. The MU maintenance strategy, which the proposed aggregates query caching mechanism is based on, outperforms all other strategies when the workload has more than 40 % insert queries. The low performance for read-intensive workloads is based on the fact, that both, the cached aggregate and the delta storage have to be queried and even an empty or small delta implies a small overhead with the current implementation.

4.3 Merge Interval

To validate the cost model for the optimal merge interval, introduced in Sect. 3.3, we have created a benchmark and compared it to our cost model. The benchmark executed a workload of 200,000 queries with 20 % selects and a varying base table size of 10 M, 20 M, and 30 M records. We have used different merge intervals with a step size of 3,000 queries starting with 1,000 and compared the best performing merge interval to the one predicted by our cost model. The results reveal that the values predicted by our cost model have a mean absolute error of 10.6 % with the remark that our approximation is limited by the chosen step size.

4.4 Object-Aware Join Operations

To evaluate the overhead of joining two tables when using the aggregates caching mechanism, we have split the single, denormalized table into a table that contains 30 M header records and a table with 311 item records. The workload as presented in Sect. 4.1 was adjusted accordingly so that the queries contain a join operation of the header and items table. With the aggregates caching mechanism, the time needed to join these two tables, divided in main and delta partitions, increases with a growing number of records in the delta storage, as shown in Table 1. Leveraging the business semantics of the chosen financial application which states that header and belonging item records are always inserted together, we can employ the object-aware join which reduces the number of necessary joins from three to one (cf. Sect. 3.4). This reduces the execution times significantly by a factor of up to 15.

Table 1. Aggregate cache execution times with join queries

Records in delta	Execution times in ms			Speedup factor
	No join	Join	Object-aware join	
0	2.69	4.01	2.95	1.36
1,000	3.24	61.87	4.39	14.10
10,000	5.32	112.89	7.81	14.46
25,000	8.79	247.29	15.65	15.80
50,000	14.58	362.40	23.85	15.20

5 Conclusions

In this paper, we have proposed a novel aggregate query caching strategy that utilizes the main-delta architecture of a columnar IMDB for efficient materialized view maintenance. Instead of invalidating or recalculating the cached query when the base data changes, we combine the cached result of the main storage with newly added records that are persisted in the delta storage. We have compared and evaluated the involved materialized view maintenance strategy to existing ones under varying workloads. Also, we have created a cost model to determine the optimal merge frequency of records in the delta storage with the main storage. To optimize the caching mechanism, we have discussed cache admission and replacement strategies, and an object-aware join mechanism. Further, we have outlined how physical updates and deletes can be handled efficiently. For evaluation, we have modeled a mixed database workload based on real customer data and the financial accounting application, revealing that our aggregates cache outperforms a simple query cache by a factor of six.

One direction of future work is the investigation of transactional properties when handling updates and deletes. Also, we plan to examine ways to persist the business semantics for object-aware join operations and to evaluate additional enterprise applications.

Acknowledgements. The authors would like to thank the SAP HANA team for the cooperation including many fruitful discussions.

References

1. Plattner, H.: A common database approach for OLTP and OLAP using an in-memory column database. In: SIGMOD (2009)
2. Plattner, H.: Sanssoucidb: an in-memory database for processing enterprise workloads. In: BTW (2011)
3. Tinnefeld, C., Müller, S., Kaltegärtner, H., Hillig, S., Butzmann, L., Eickhoff, D., Klauck, S., Taschik, D., Wagner, B., Xylander, O., Zeier, A., Plattner, H., Tosun, C.: Available-to-promise on an in-memory column store. In: BTW, pp. 667–686 (2011)
4. Gupta, A., Mumick, I.S., et al.: Maintenance of materialized views: problems, techniques, and applications. Data Eng. Bull. **18**(2), 3–18 (1995)
5. Blakeley, J.A., Larson, P.A., Tompa, F.W.: Efficiently updating materialized views. In: SIGMOD (1986)
6. Agrawal, D., El Abbadi, A., Singh, A., Yurek, T.: Efficient view maintenance at data warehouses. In: SIGMOD (1997)
7. Bello, R.G., Dias, K., Downing, A., Feenan, J., Finnerty, J., Norcott, W.D., Sun, H., Witkowski, A., Ziauddin, M.: Materialized views in oracle. In: VLDB (1998)
8. Zhou, J., Larson, P.A., Elmongui, H.G.: Lazy maintenance of materialized views. In: VLDB (2007)
9. Zhuge, Y., Garcia-Molina, H., Hammer, J., Widom, J.: View maintenance in a warehousing environment. In: SIGMOD (1995)
10. Jain, H., Gosain, A.: A comprehensive study of view maintenance approaches in data warehousing evolution. SIGSOFT **37**(5), 1–8 (2012)
11. Färber, F., Cha, S.K., Primsch, J., Bornhövd, C., Sigg, S., Lehner, W.: SAP HANA database: data management for modern business applications. In: SIGMOD (2011)
12. Kemper, A., Neumann, T.: Hyper: a hybrid OLTP and OLAP main memory database system based on virtual memory snapshots. In: ICDE (2011)
13. Grund, M., Krüger, J., Plattner, H., Zeier, A., Cudre-Mauroux, P., Madden, S.: Hyrise: a main memory hybrid storage engine. In: VLDB (2010)
14. Abadi, D., Madden, S., Ferreira, M.: Integrating compression and execution in column-oriented database systems. In: SIGMOD (2006)
15. Krueger, J., Kim, C., Grund, M., Satish, N., Schwalb, D., Chhugani, J., Plattner, H., Dubey, P., Zeier, A.: Fast updates on read-optimized databases using multi-core CPUs. In: VLDB (2012)

16. Plattner, H., Zeier, A.: In-Memory Data Management: An Inflection Point for Enterprise Applications. Springer, Heidelberg (2011)
17. Buneman, O.P., Clemons, E.K.: Efficiently monitoring relational databases. ACM Trans. Database Syst. 4(3), 368–382 (1979)
18. Mumick, I.S., Quass, D., Mumick, B.S.: Maintenance of data cubes and summary tables in a warehouse. In: SIGMOD (1997)
19. Gray, J., Bosworth, A.: Data cube: a relational aggregation operator generalizing GROUP-BY, CROSS-TAB, and SUB-TOTALS. In: ICDE (1996)
20. Schaffner, J., Eckart, B., Jacobs, D., Schwarz, C., Plattner, H., Zeier, A.: Predicting in-memory database performance for automating cluster management tasks. In: ICDE (2011)
21. Manegold, S., Boncz, P., Kersten, M.: Generic database cost models for hierarchical memory systems. In: VLDB (2002)
22. Cole, R., Funke, F., Giakoumakis, L., Guy, W., Kemper, A., Krompass, S., Kuno, H., Nambiar, R., Neumann, T., Poess, M., Sattler, K.U., Seibold, M., Simon, E., Waas, F.: The mixed workload CH-benCHmark. In: DBTest (2011)

An Evaluation of Strict Timestamp Ordering Concurrency Control for Main-Memory Database Systems

Stephan Wolf, Henrik Mühe$^{(\boxtimes)}$, Alfons Kemper, and Thomas Neumann

Technische Universität München, Munich, Germany
{wolfst,muehe,kemper,neumann}@in.tum.de

Abstract. With the fundamental change of hardware technology, main-memory database systems have emerged as the next generation of DBMS. Thus, new methods to execute transactions in a serial, lock-free mode have been investigated and successfully employed, for instance in H-Store or HyPer. Although these techniques allow for unprecedentedly high throughput for suitable workloads, their throughput quickly diminishes once unsuitable transactions, for instance those crossing partition borders, are encountered. Still, little research concentrates on the overdue re-evaluation of traditional techniques, that do not rely on partitioning.

This paper studies strict timestamp ordering (STO), a "good old" technique, in the context of modern main-memory database systems built on commodity hardware with high memory capacities. We show that its traditional main drawback – slowing down reads – has a much lower impact in a main-memory setting than in traditional disk-based DBMS. As a result, STO is a competitive concurrency control method which outperforms the partitioned execution approach, for example in the TPC-C benchmark, as soon as a certain percentage of the workload crosses partition boundaries.

1 Introduction

In recent years, hardware with large capacities of main memory has become available, leading to a renewed interest in main-memory database systems. Here, page faults no longer need to be compensated by executing parallel transactions, which allows for removing many synchronization components that are indispensable in traditional, disk-based database systems. Harizopoulos et al. [HAMS08] found, that most time spent executing a transaction is actually used by components like buffer manager, lock manager and latching.

Without the need for hiding I/O latencies, other execution paradigms like partitioned serial execution, as first investigated by Kallman et al. [KKN+08] in their H-Store prototype, become viable alternatives to traditional locking. Here, transactions are executed sequentially on each partition of the data without the need for any concurrency control at all.

Even though a sequential execution approach leads to outstanding performance when the data and workload allow for partitioning in a suitable way

© Springer International Publishing Switzerland 2015
A. Jagatheesan et al. (Eds.): IMDM 2013/2014, LNCS 8921, pp. 82–93, 2015.
DOI: 10.1007/978-3-319-13960-9_7

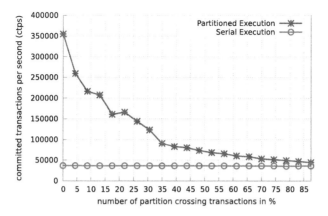

Fig. 1. Throughput decrease related to the ratio of part partition-crossing transactions.

[KKN+08,KN11], partition crossing transactions quickly lead to a deterioration in throughput, even on a single node without additional network delays (see Fig. 1). One reason is that current implementations often rely on coarse granularity synchronization mechanisms, like the full database lock used in the HyPer DBMS prototype [KN11].

In this paper, we reinvestigate the "good old" timestamp-based concurrency control as suggested in [BHG87,Car83] decades ago. Major drawbacks of the timestamp approach – like having to write a timestamp for every read – have to be re-evaluated when data resides in main-memory.

The remainder of this paper is structured as follows: In Sect. 2, we will introduce both partitioned serial execution, as well as the strict timestamp ordering approach (STO) evaluated in this work. Section 3 describes our implementation of STO inside the HyPer database system prototype and highlights the most severe adjustments required when using timestamp-based concurrency control mechanisms. We offer a thorough evaluation of STO, as well as a comparison of STO with partitioned serial execution in Sect. 4. Section 5 concludes this paper.

2   Formal Background

Before discussing the implementation of strict timestamp ordering in HyPer, we will provide the theoretical background of the algorithm. Additionally, we outline serial execution and partitioned execution, which we will compare to strict timestamp ordering.

2.1   Serial Execution

Traditional disk-based database systems frequently rely on locking to achieve serializability among concurrent transactions. When reading or writing data to disk, this is essential since I/O latency need to be masked. In main-memory database systems, however, the need for masking I/O misses no longer exists allowing for the efficient serial execution of suitable workloads without traditional concurrency control.

H-Store [KKN+08] pioneered the idea of removing buffer management, as well as locking and latching from main-memory database systems, allowing for the efficient execution of partitionable workloads with minimal overhead. This concept, which we refer to as *serial execution*, has since been picked up by other main-memory database systems, for instance the commercialized version of H-Store named VoltDB [Vol10] as well as our HyPer research prototype DBMS [KN11].

Unlike VoltDB, HyPer also supports mixed OLTP/OLAP applications by separating the two disparate workloads using virtual memory snapshotting [MKN11]. Here, we concentrate only on the OLTP synchronization.

2.2   Partitioned Execution

Scaling the transactional throughput when using serial execution is possible by running multiple serial execution threads in parallel for disjoint partitions of the data. As shown by Curino et al. [CZJM10], some workloads can be partitioned such that cases where a transaction has to access multiple partitions are rare. For the TPC-C benchmark[1], for instance, only 12.5 % of all transactions access more than one partition of the data.

Other main memory database systems, which rely on partitioning, disallow the execution of transactions which might access more than one partition of the data. In contrast, HyPer executes transactions assuming that they will operate on only one data partition. If a transaction accesses data outside its own partition, a database lock is acquired causing transactional processing to fall back into serial execution mode without concurrency on separate partitions. After the transaction has finished, the database lock is released and concurrent execution on all partitions of the database is resumed. We call this execution mode *partitioned execution* or *PE* for short.

2.3   Strict Timestamp Ordering (STO)

Timestamp-based concurrency control uses timestamps for synchronization instead of locks. From the outside it seems that the transactions are executed sequentially according to their starting time. In other words, the scheduler generates serializable schedules that are equal to the serial execution of the transactions ordered by their starting time.

To achieve this, the transaction manager assigns a timestamp $TS(T_i)$ to each transaction T_i at its start and guarantees that the timestamp of transactions that started later is always higher than the timestamps of all earlier transactions. These timestamps are used to guarantee the *Timestamp Ordering (TO)* rule: if two operations $p_i(x)$ and $q_j(x)$ are in conflict, i.e. they access the

---

[1] See http://www.tpc.org/tpcc/.

same tuple x and at least one operation is a write operation, then the operation of the transaction with the lower timestamp is always executed first. Thereby, the resulting schedule is equal to the serial execution of the transactions ordered by their timestamp and, as a consequence, it is serializable.

In order to enforce the TO rule, the database system has to save the timestamp of the transaction which has last read tuple x, and the timestamp of the transaction which has last changed tuple x. In the following, these timestamps are denoted as $readTS(x)$ and $writeTS(x)$.

With these meta data, the transaction manager is able to perform the following test, which enforces the TO rule:

1. $r_i(x)$: T_i wants to read x:
   (a) If $TS(T_i) < writeTS(x)$, the TO rule would be violated. Thus, the transaction T_i has to be aborted.
   (b) Otherwise, allow access and set
       $readTS(x) := max(TS(T_i), readTS(x))$.
2. $w_i(x)$: T_i wants to write x:
   (a) If $TS(T_i) < readTS(x)$ or $TS(T_i) < writeTS(x)$,
       the TO rule would be violated. Thus, the transaction T_i has to be aborted.
   (b) Otherwise, allow access and set $writeTS(A) := TS(T_i)$.

It is required that write operations on the same data tuple are executed atomically and write and read operations are mutually excluded.

According to [BHG87] and [CS84], this algorithm is called *Basic Timestamp Ordering (BTO)*. It generates serializable schedules, but does not guarantee recoverability. In fact, aborted transactions can cause inconsistency, as another transaction which accessed dirty data could already be committed.

As recoverability is essential for database systems, we employ an extension of Basic Timestamp Ordering called *Strict Timestamp Ordering (STO)* [BHG87]. STO does not only provide recoverable schedules, but also strict schedules. That means, that no uncommitted changes of a running transaction are overwritten or read by another transaction. This is prevented by the use of a dirty bit. Each transaction marks tuples with uncommitted changes by setting the dirty bit and other transactions accessing such a tuple have to wait until the dirty bit is unset, which happens when the previous transaction commits or is rolled back. In order to avoid deadlocks, the transaction manager has to ensure that a transaction never waits for younger transactions. Thereby, cyclic waiting is prevented, which is one of the necessary Coffman conditions for a deadlock [CES71].

3   Implementation of STO

In order to evaluate the performance of STO, we used the database system HyPer [KN11] to implement the described algorithm. HyPer is an in-memory, high-performance hybrid OLTP and OLAP DBMS that originally relies on sequential execution for transaction processing. To further improve transaction processing throughput, transactions are not interpreted but are compiled to machine code using the LLVM compiler back-end. This removes interpretation overhead at runtime and improves hardware optimizations, for example branch prediction [Neu11].

The implementation of STO in HyPer required not only a new transaction manager, but also architectural modifications because of concurrency inside partitions. These impacts of STO on the architecture will be described in Sect. 3.2. Before that, the basic data structures needed by the STO implementation are presented to provide a better understanding of the implementation.

3.1   Data Structures

Besides the read and write timestamps, further data structures were necessary. To avoid that dirty data is read or overwritten, a dirty bit is needed. Furthermore, because of reasons presented in Sect. 3.2.1, our implementation requires a delete flag. And last but not least, a dirty bit inventory was needed, which is responsible for unsetting the dirty bits after a transaction has aborted or committed.

3.1.1   Timestamp Codes

We used 32-bit values for the read and write timestamps and encoded the dirty bit and delete flag into the write timestamp. The highest bit is reserved for the dirty bit and the delete flag is set when all other 31 bits of the write timestamp are set. This design has two advantages compared to a separate delete flag and dirty bit:

- As the write timestamp has to be checked anyway, the check for the dirty bit does not require an additional memory operation. Furthermore, checking if the dirty bit is not set and the write timestamp is lower than the transaction's timestamp requires only one arithmetic operation.
- The delete flag design is beneficial, as it makes a separate check for tuple deletion unnecessary. When the delete flag is set, the write timestamp is equal to the highest possible timestamp. So, all transactions accessing the deleted tuple will abort without an additional check of the delete flag.

As the transactions' timestamps have to be assigned in strictly increasing order, the size of the timestamp variables determines when the timestamp arrays have to be reset. If a database processes 250 000 transactions per second in a lab setting (in almost every real-world scenario, this throughput is not required), the timestamps would have to be reset only after approximately 2 h.

This can be done as follows: When a new transaction is started and acquires a new timestamp, it is checked if the value range is exceeded. If this is the case, all running transactions are rolled back, all timestamp fields are reset, and the aborted transactions are restarted. The impact of aborting running transactions is negligible, as the length of OLTP transactions is short. For domains, where a short and rare delay during transaction processing is not tolerable, 64-bit timestamps can be used.

3.1.2 Dirty Bit Inventory

The dirty bit inventory is necessary for resetting the dirty bits and is maintained for each running transaction. Whenever a transaction sets the dirty bit of a tuple which was not set before, the tuple identifier is inserted into the transaction's dirty bit inventory. After a transaction aborts or commits, the dirty bit inventory is processed and the transaction's dirty bits are unset. As a tuple identifier is only ever inserted once into the dirty bit inventory and as each tuple identifier cannot be in two dirty bit inventories of different transactions at the same time, it need not be checked whether the dirty bit is set and originates from the current transaction, which simplifies resetting the dirty bit.

3.2 Architectural Details

By contrast to partitioned execution, strict timestamp ordering allows multiple concurrent transactions inside partitions. We will briefly discuss the necessary architectural adaption in this section.

3.2.1 Undoing Deletes

One problem is that concurrency on partition level could violate recoverability. When a transaction aborts, all its effects have to be undone. If the transaction has deleted tuples, they have to be reinserted. However, this could fail in a naive implementation because of violations of unique keys, if a concurrent transaction has inserted a tuple with the same key in the meantime.

We solved this problem by deferring the removal of tuples to the commit phase of a transaction. Deleted tuples are marked with the delete flag and the dirty bit is set, so that other transactions trying to access this tuple will wait. The deleting transaction skips this tuple the next time it tries to access it.

3.2.2 Index Structures and Synchronization

Index structures need to be refitted to support concurrent access. Optimizing index structures for concurrency is an active and complex topic of research. Transactional memory implementations [DFGG11, DGK09], as well as relativistic programming [TMW10, HW10] provide promising results on modern hardware.

In our implementation, we use full index latching to synchronize access to index structures. This is reasonable, as each partition has its own index structures. However, when done naively, this solution can constitute a major performance bottleneck as shown by [HAMS08], who analyzed the overhead of traditional locking in the context of main-memory database systems. We evaded this issue by optimizing the lock implementation. Concretely, we used an adapted version of the MCS lock [MCS91], which uses spinning on thread-local variables for waiting and allows reader and writer synchronization. That boost the performance of our STO implementation by a factor of two compared to traditional latching using the lock implementation from the `pthreads` library. Furthermore, we avoid locking the index structures for each tuple. Instead, if we subsequently access tuples from the same partition, we keep the lock until we switch to the next partition.

3.2.3 Synchronization of Admissibility Check

Besides the index structures, we also have to ensure that the check for admissibility of a transaction's operation is thread-safe. As we have to mutually exclude access to the index structures, we avoiding the necessity of additional locking, by extending this critical section to also contain the check of admissibility. Concretely, when accessing a tuple from one partition, we lock its index structures, lookup the tuple, perform the admissibility check and access the tuple. Before switching to the next partition, we release the lock, so that other transactions can proceed working on that partition. Access to the dirty bit inventory does not need to be synchronized, as each transaction has its own inventory.

4 Evaluation

In this Section, we will evaluate the strict timestamp ordering approach and compare its performance to partitioned serial execution. All benchmarks were conducted on a Dell PowerEdge R910 server with 4x Intel Xeon X7560 processors each containing eight cores clocked at 2.26 GHz. The server is equipped with 1 TB of main-memory split into 64×16 GB RDIMMs connected to four separate memory controllers interconnected by Intel's Quick Path Interconnect technology. For our evaluation, redo logging was disabled for all approaches, to ensure that the results are not distorted by effects resulting from the logging technique we use.

4.1 Read versus Write Performance

One reason, why STO performed poorly on disk-resident database systems, is that it significantly slowed down read operations: Updating the read timestamp caused additional disk latency. In memory resident database systems, I/O latency is not dominating the performance any more. Therefore, we re-evaluated the read performance of STO.

For this, we designed a microbenchmark. It consists of one large table with 10 million tuples. Each tuple consists of two attributes: a 64-bit integer *key* and a 64-bit integer *value*. A hash map is used as primary index. The table is divided into 128 partitions by using Fibonacci hashing on the primary key. To avoid conflicts, each thread has its own set of tuples, which we call the threads *workset*. Concretely, the first thread accesses only the first $\lfloor 10\ million/(number\ of\ threads)\rfloor$ tuples, the second thread the following $\lfloor 10\ million/(number\ of\ threads)\rfloor$ tuples, etc.

The benchmark offers two modes: read or write. In both modes, there is only one type of transaction that is provided with an array of 50 primary keys taken from the threads workset. In write mode, the transactions increment the *value* attribute of the corresponding tuples and in read mode, the transactions fetch

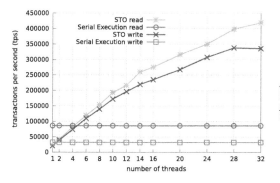

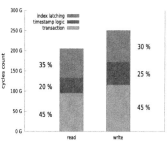

Fig. 2. The read and write performance of STO   **Fig. 3.** Cycles distribution

the *value* attribute of each tuple and check a condition, that is always false, to avoid that the query optimizer removes the fetch query, as the value is not used.

As the partitions are arranged by the Fibonacci hash of the primary key, the workset of each thread is uniformly distributed over all partitions. This has two implications: First, all transactions are partition-crossing. Second, the transactions interfere with each other by latching the partitions' index structures. But they do not conflict, as the data sets are disjoint.

Figure 2 shows the results from the micro benchmark subject to the number of threads. The duration of processing 1 million transactions was measured and the transactions per second (tps) throughput determined. Three runs were executed for each measurement and the mean was taken.

STO's read and write curve both start nearly with the same throughput. The slope exhibits linear growth up to 16 threads. Each additional thread constantly increases the throughput by about 20 000 tps. Starting from 16 threads, the system uses hyper-threading to execute the software threads. As a result, the gradient slowly declines and the throughput increase gained by adding a new thread declines with each additional thread. Still the throughput increases at a slower rate of about 10 000 tps on average.

Looking at write performance, STO can outperform serial execution when using at least 2 threads. Furthermore, by using 32 threads, we can increase the throughput by one order of magnitude compared to the serial execution.

In read mode, STO achieves about 25 % higher peak throughput than in write mode. In contrast, serial execution achieves a difference of a factor of 2.5. This shows that the traditional problem of STO – slowing down read operations – still persists in main-memory database systems but its impact is reduced: While in disk-resident database systems the difference between read and write operations was about one order of magnitude because of disk latency, in main-memory database systems, the difference is about a factor of 2 to 3.

4.2   Overhead Analysis

As it was shown by Harizopoulos et al. [HAMS08] that latching in traditional database systems produces severe overhead, we employed a lock implementation that is optimized for highly parallel systems, called the MCS lock. Still, we should differentiate between the overhead produced by the STO logic and the overhead produced by latching, as STO does not rely on latching index structures. For example, lock-free index structures or index structures which rely on relativistic programming [HW10, TMW10] could be used.

We analyzed how much time is needed for each component of the concurrency control approach: Latching, STO logic and execution of the transaction itself using the previous benchmark in both modes. For determining the time difference between two evaluation points, we used the CPU cycles counter. Concretely, we defined measure points before and after each latching operation as well as each STO operation. At these points, the difference between the current cycles count and the cycles count at the previous measure point is computed and the result is added to a thread-local summation variable for each phase.

Figure 3 shows the resulting distribution taken from one run with 32 threads. Similar results were obtained when using a different number of threads and are therefore omitted here. It can be observed that the total cycles count of the write transactions is about 25 % higher than of the read transaction, which matches the result from the write and read comparison.

Furthermore, in both cases, the basic transaction instructions such as updating tuples, fetching tuples, etc., cover about half of the time of a transaction. In read mode, this does not seem to fit to the previous benchmark, where serial execution was about 4 times faster than STO run with a single thread. Concretely, the time needed for the basic transaction instructions should be about one quarter of the cycles total. The reason for this difference can be explained by cache effects. When, for example, a timestamp is updated, the changes will be written into the processor's cache. As a result, the expensive propagation of the change to the main-memory will happen, when the cache line is replaced, which is usually caused by a read operation. As the basic transaction instructions are read intensive – looking up primary keys in the hash map, fetching tuples – they are likely to replace cache lines and cause costly propagation to main-memory. As a consequence, the expensive write operations caused by latching or timestamp maintenance slow down the basic transaction instructions, as these are read intensive. Therefore, half of the overhead of the basic transaction instructions seems to be also caused by locking and latching. In write mode, this effect is not significant. Here, the analysis reflects the results of the previous benchmark: When using one thread STO achieves about half of the performance of serial execution.

The overhead caused by concurrency control is distributed similarly in read and write mode. Although the STO overhead in write mode is higher than in read mode – the dirty bit inventory has to be processed and the dirty bits have to be reset – it can be observed that in both cases index latching causes more overhead than the STO logic itself. Nevertheless the optimized MCS lock could decrease

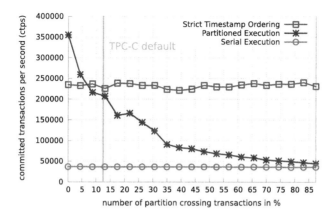

Fig. 4. TPC-C benchmark with varying the number of partition-crossing transactions

the overhead of latching by about a factor of 4 compared to the results of running a disk-resident database in main-memory [HAMS08]. Still, index latching produces significant overhead and we will investigate the performance improvements achievable with lock free index structures in future research.

4.3   Strict Timestamp Ordering versus Partitioned Execution

Finally, we compare strict timestamp ordering to partitioned execution while varying the number of partition crossing transactions. For the analysis, we used the well-known TPC-C benchmark (See Footnote 1) as it is easily partitionable by using the warehouse id and widely used as a benchmark for main-memory database systems comparable to HyPer, for instance in [KKN+08, Vol10].

In the TPC-C benchmark there are two types of transactions that cross partition borders – 25 % of the *payment* transactions and 10 % of the *new order* transactions. Regarding their ratio in the total workload, this leads to a total of about 12.5 % partition-crossing transactions. For this benchmark, we equally adjusted the percentage of partition-crossing *payment* and *new order* transactions from 0 % to 100 %, resulting in a total ratio of 0 % to 87.5 %.

In Fig. 4, we show the average sustainable throughput of serial execution, partitioned execution and strict timestamp ordering while varying the percentage of transactions which cross partition boundaries. In order to provide a fair comparison, we counted only the number of committed transactions per second, as STO solves conflicts by aborting the conflicting transaction. We set the number of warehouses to 128, which resulted in about 17 GB of data, and used 20 threads.

When no partition crossing transactions are included in the workload, PE performs significantly better than STO. Here, conditions are optimal for PE as every transaction is restricted to one partition of the data and no locking is necessary at all. STO, on the other hand, requires atomic operations for locking and needs to update read/write timestamps. Therefore, the throughput achieved by STO is about 33 % lower than the throughput of PE.

For an increased number of partition crossing transactions, PE's throughput declines significantly. At 12.5 % partition crossing transactions – the percentage in the original TPC-C – the throughput achieved by PE has already dropped below the throughput achieved with STO. As the number of partition crossing transactions increases further, the throughput curve converges to the throughput achieved by serial execution. This was to be expected, since PE uses serial execution without parallelism for partition crossing transactions causing it to behave like serial execution for high percentages of partition crossing transactions.

STO exhibits constant throughput regardless of how many transactions cross partition borders. This is due to its reliance on per-tuple timestamps which (a) constitutes a fine-granularity concurrency control method and (b) does not require a centralized locking infrastructure. Thus, it is perfectly suited for workloads that can not be completely partitioned.

5   Conclusion

In this paper, we re-evaluated the traditional strict timestamp ordering concurrency control algorithm in a main-memory database system on modern hardware, while most modern main-memory DBMS omit explicit concurrency control in favor of partitioning and serial execution.

We found that the traditional drawback of STO – slowing down read operations as if they were write operations – is less significant in main-memory than in disk-based database systems. Here, the performance of read and write operations differs by about a factor of 2, whereas in disk-resident database systems the difference was at least one order of magnitude because of disk latency.

As a result, STO is a competitive alternative to partitioned execution: While partitioned execution is – by design – ideal for a perfectly partitionable workload, STO allows the efficient execution of workloads regardless of the quality of the underlying partitioning. Even a low number of partition-crossing transactions, for example the default ratio of 12.5 % partition crossing transactions in the TPC-C benchmark, suffice that STO outperforms PE. Therefore, STO is suitable for environments where transactions can not be easily restricted to work on only one partition of the data.

Additionally, we found that traditional bottlenecks like latching need to be re-evaluated from an implementation standpoint: We could improve the performance of STO by a factor of 2 by using an optimized latch implementation which uses thread-local spinning. Still, the overhead of latching stays a significant factor and it should be evaluated if technologies like lock-free index structures, transactional memory or relativistic programming can further reduce it.

In summary, re-investigating the suitability of traditional works in concurrency control for their performance in a fundamentally changed hardware environment has allowed us to find a more robust concurrency control method for main memory DBMS that is competitive to current approaches.

References

[BHG87]   Bernstein, P.A., Hadzilacos, V., Goodman, N.: Concurrency Control and Recovery in Database Systems. Addison-Wesley, New York (1987)

[Car83]   Carey, M.J.: Modeling and evaluation of database concurrency control algorithms. Ph.D. thesis, University of California, Berkeley (1983)

[CES71]   Coffman, E.G., Elphick, M., Shoshani, A.: System deadlocks. ACM Comput. Surv. **3**(2), 67–78 (1971)

[CS84]   Carey, M.J., Stonebraker, M.: The performance of concurrency control algorithms for database management systems. In: Proceedings of the 10th International Conference on Very Large Data Bases, VLDB 1984, pp. 107–118. Morgan Kaufmann Publishers, San Francisco (1984)

[CZJM10] Curino, C., Zhang, Y., Jones, E.P.C., Madden, S.: Schism: a workload-driven approach to database replication and partitioning. PVLDB **3**(1), 48–57 (2010)

[DFGG11] Dragojević, A., Felber, P., Gramoli, V., Guerraoui, R.: Why STM can be more than a Research Toy. Commun. ACM **54**, 70–77 (2011)

[DGK09]   Dragojević, A., Guerraoui, R., Kapalka, M.: Stretching transactional memory. ACM SIGPLAN Not. **44**, 155–165 (2009)

[HAMS08] Harizopoulos, S., Abadi, D.J., Madden, S., Stonebraker, M.: OLTP through the looking glass, and what we found there. In: Proceedings of the 2008 ACM SIGMOD International Conference on Management of Data, pp. 981–992. ACM Press, New York (2008)

[HW10]   Howard, P.W., Walpole, J.: Relativistic red-black trees. Technical report. PSU Computer Science Department, Portland, Oregon, USA (2010)

[KKN+08] Kallman, R., et al.: A high-performance, distributed main memory transaction processing system. PVLDB **1**(2), 1496–1499 (2008)

[KN11]   Kemper, A., Neumann, T.: HyPer: a hybrid OLTP&OLAP main memory database system based on virtual memory snapshots. In: ICDE, pp. 195–206 (2011)

[MCS91]   Mellor-Crummey, J.M., Scott, M.L.: Algorithms for scalable synchronization on shared-memory multiprocessors. ACM Trans. Comput. Syst. **9**(1), 21–65 (1991)

[MKN11]   Mühe, H., Kemper, A., Neumann, T.: How to efficiently snapshot transactional data: hardware or software controlled? In: DaMoN, pp. 17–26 (2011)

[Neu11]   Neumann, T.: Efficiently compiling efficient query plans for modern hardware. PVLDB **4**(9), 539–550 (2011)

[TMW10]   Triplett, J., McKenney, P.E., Walpole, J.: Scalable concurrent hash tables via relativistic programming. ACM SIGOPS Oper. Syst. Rev. **44**(3), 102–109 (2010)

[Vol10]   VoltDB LLC. VoltDB technical overview (2010). http://voltdb.com/_pdf/VoltDBTechnicalOverviewWhitePaper.pdf

IMDM 2014 Workshop Papers

Database Scan Variants on Modern CPUs: A Performance Study

David Broneske[1]([✉]), Sebastian Breß[1,2], and Gunter Saake[1]

[1] University of Magdeburg, Magdeburg, Germany
{david.broneske,gunter.saake}@ovgu.de,
sebastian.bress@cs.tu-dortmund.de
[2] TU Dortmund University, Dortmund, Germany

Abstract. Main-memory databases rely on highly tuned database operations to achieve peak performance. Recently, it has been shown that different code optimizations for database operations favor different processors. However, it is still not clear how the combination of code optimizations (e.g., loop unrolling and vectorization) will affect the performance of database algorithms on different processors.

In this paper, we extend prior studies by an in-depth performance analysis of different variants of the scan operator. We find that the performance of the scan operator for different processors gets even harder to predict when multiple code optimizations are combined. Since the scan is the most simple database operator, we expect the same effects for more complex operators such as joins. Based on these results, we identify practical problems for a query processor and discuss how we can counter these challenges in future work.

1 Introduction

Operators in a main-memory database are heavily tuned to meet performance needs of tomorrow. In the past, tuning operators for the underlying hardware has attracted much attention (e.g., implementing different join strategies [1–3]). Due to ever-increasing capabilities of modern CPUs (e.g., an increasing number of cores, size of caches, and width of vector registers), the behavior of database algorithms is hard to predict on a given machine [2].

Code optimizations, such as *loop unrolling* or *vectorization*, have different impacts on the performance depending on the given workload (e.g., selectivity) and processor [17]. Furthermore, considering the combination of different code optimizations, algorithm performance will get even more unpredictable, because of interactions between optimizations. In this paper, we perform a first experimental study on the performance impact of combined optimizations. We restrict our study to scans, because it is a very simple operator, where it is feasible to implement a high number of variants.

In our in-depth performance analysis, we analyze the impact of four common code optimizations – loop unrolling, branch-free code, vectorization, and parallelization – and *all* of their combinations. Thus, we contribute in this paper:

© Springer International Publishing Switzerland 2015
A. Jagatheesan et al. (Eds.): IMDM 2013/2014, LNCS 8921, pp. 97–111, 2015.
DOI: 10.1007/978-3-319-13960-9_8

1. A performance comparison of scan variants on different processors for varying workloads (e.g., selectivity and data volume)
2. A description of the relation between hardware characteristics and code optimizations for the scan operator

As a result, we discover that the optimal variant of the scan operator for a given workload is very likely to change across different processors.

Most importantly, there is no simple dependency between the properties of the hardware and the optimal scan operator, because a combined set of optimizations *interact* with each other. The variability in workloads, machines, and sets of code optimizations leads to a large optimization space for database systems and is an unused optimization potential that has not yet been considered to its whole extent. As a consequence, we argue that query execution engines should exploit these unused potentials.

The remainder of this paper is structured as follows. In the next section, we introduce four common code optimizations and present how we applied the optimizations on a simple scan operator in Sect. 3. We evaluate our scan variants on different machines and state important findings in Sect. 4. In Sect. 5, we discuss the impact of our results. We present related work in Sect. 6 and conclude our work in Sect. 7.

2 Code Optimizations

In this section, we discuss basics of the four common code optimizations that we apply on the scan operator, namely branch-free code, loop unrolling, vectorization, and parallelization. These code optimizations improve either pipeline or data parallelism to exploit different capabilities of modern CPUs [6]. Of course, there are numerous more code optimizations, such as loop fission, or full computation [7,17], but we limit them to a practically applicable subset in this work.

2.1 Branching vs. No-Branching

The usual way to include conditions in a program is to use if-statements. However, when the processor is filling its instruction pipeline, it has to decide whether to include an instruction which depends on the branch or to omit it. For this, CPUs use branch prediction to estimate the result of the branch condition. However, if the outcome of a branch is constantly changing (e.g., in a selection with 50 % selectivity), branch prediction often fails and the pipeline has to be flushed and refilled, which reduces instruction throughput.

As a consequence of the pitfalls of branching, a possible optimization is to write the code in a way that it does not contain any branches. A possible example is to use predication for selections [16]. Although omitting branches avoids branch mispredictions – and, thus, pipeline flushes – we need to execute more instructions than necessary. Thus, it may only be helpful for if-statements whose outcome is hard to predict.

2.2   Loop Unrolling

Loop unrolling is a well-known technique to reduce pipeline stalls in tight for-loops [9]. If a for-loop consists of a small amount of instructions (e.g., initializing an array: $array[i] = i$) the overhead of the instructions of the loop may deteriorate its whole performance. Thus, instead of having just one initialization for loop counter i inside the loop body, we could replicate the body to also initialize the array entries of $i + 1$, $i + 2$, and $i + 3$. With this, we reduce stalls in the pipeline of the processor [9], but increase the code size, which may lead to a higher miss-rate in the instruction cache. Notably, modern compilers feature automatic unrolling of loops. Nevertheless, an adaptive unrolling which depends on the number of iterations in the loops cannot be achieved, because the number of iterations is often unknown at compile-time.

2.3   Vectorization

The ability to execute a single instruction on multiple data items (called *SIMD*) is an important property of modern CPUs to improve data parallelism. Their benefit has already been shown for applications such as database operations [22] and compression techniques in combination with database scans [19,20]. These SIMD registers offer small load and store latencies [22] and execute one instruction on several data items, for instance, four 32-bit integer values. Since compilers are sometimes not able to vectorize instructions themselves [22], special compiler intrinsics (e.g., *SSE* instructions) are used to explicitly exploit SIMD functionality.

2.4   Parallelization

Modern CPUs can execute several threads in parallel. Thus, exploiting thread parallelism in a database is of high importance for improving its performance [12]. Parallelizing database operations implies that data can be partitioned over several threads which work in parallel to achieve lower response times. However, the results of each thread have to be combined to form the end result making parallelization less beneficial for big result sizes. Furthermore, for small jobs, the overhead of coordinating the threads may consume the benefit of parallelization [18].

3   Variants for Database Scans

For the implementation of the database scan variants, we chose the database management system CoGaDB (*Column-oriented GPU-accelerated DBMS* [5]) which already offers the basic variants of the scan operator. Hence, we only had to extend this operator set by the combination of optimizations. For simplicity, we present an excerpt of supported types and predicates of a database scan, which we limit here to predicates of the form $x < c$, where c is a constant. Our implemented scan extracts a position list with the tuple identifiers of matching tuples. Of course, this is only one variant of a scan and other approaches of a scan such as extracting a bitmap from the input are worth to evaluate in future work.

3.1   Implementation of Single Optimizations

The simple serial implementation of the scan is straightforward; we sketch the code in Listing 1.1. The main component of the serial scan is the for-loop which iterates over the input **array** of size *array_size*.

```
1   for(int i = 0; i < array_size; ++i) {
2       SELECTION_BODY(array,comp_val,i,result,pos,<);
3   }
```

Listing 1.1. Serial scan for comparator less than.

Inside the for-loop, we use a macro (cf. Listing 1.2) to be able to switch the code between branching and branch-free code during compile time. Both macros evaluate whether the array value is smaller than the comparison value **comp_val**, and if true, it writes the position **pos** into the array **result**.

Using these macros allows to either have a branch in the code that conditionally inserts the positions into the positionlist, or else to have a branch-free version of the conditional insertion. In fact, the branch-free version has a stable number of executed instructions and, thus, no branch mispredictions can happen, which increases instruction throughput. Nevertheless, if the comparison is often evaluated as false, we incur an overhead compared to the code with branches.

```
1   #define SELECTION_BODY_BRANCH(array,value,i,result,pos,COMPARATOR) if(array[i]
        COMPARATOR value){result[pos++]=i;}
2   #define SELECTION_BODY_NOBRANCH(array,value,i,result,pos,COMPARATOR) result[pos]=i;
        pos+=(array[i] COMPARATOR value);
```

Listing 1.2. Macros for branching or branch-free code.

Apart from code with or without branching, another possible variant can be generated by unrolling the loop. In Listing 1.3, we sketch the schema for unrolling the macro inside the loop. The exact code depends on the number of unrolled loop bodies k and has to be implemented for every k that has to be supported in the scan. Notably, each variant of the unrolled scan is also available with branch-free code, since we can use the same macro as in the simple serial scan.

```
1   for(int i = 0; i < array_size; i+=k) {
2       SELECTION_BODY(array,comp_val,i,result,pos,<);
3       ...
4       SELECTION_BODY(array,comp_val,i+(k−1),result,pos,<);
5   }
6   ... //process remaining tuples in a normal loop
```

Listing 1.3. k-times loop-unrolled serial scan.

Apart from reducing pipeline stalls by using loop unrolling, our next serial variant uses SSE intrinsics to implement vectorization. Our algorithm in Listing 1.4 is based on the SIMD scan by Zhou and Ross [22]. Since SIMD operations work on 16-byte aligned memory, we first have to process tuples that are not aligned. For this, we use the serial variant, since only a few tuples have to be processed. The same procedure is executed for the remaining tuples that do not completely fill one SIMD register. The presented code snippet evaluates the elements of an SIMD array and retrieves a bit mask for each comparison (cf. Line 4). After that, the mask is evaluated for the four data items and if there is a match, the corresponding position is inserted into the position list (cf. Line 6–10). Notably, similar to the algorithm by Zhou and Ross, we also use an if statement for evaluating whether there has been a match at all, which could reduce executed instructions if the selectivity is high.

```
1  ... // Code for unaligned tuples
2  for(int i=0;i < simd_array_size;++i)
3  {
4    mask=SIMD_COMPARISON(SIMD_array[i],
         comp_val);
5    if(mask){
6      for (int j=0;j < SIMD_Length;++j)
7      {
8        if((mask >> j) & 1)
9          result_array[pos++]=j+offsets;
10       }
11     }
12 }
13 ... // Code for remaining tuples
```

Listing 1.4. Vectorized serial scan.

```
1  //build local result in parallel
2  for(int i=0;i < num_of_threads;++i) {
3    do parallel: serial_selection(...);
4  }
5  //build prefix sum
6  prefix_sum[0]=0;
7  for(int i=0;i < num_of_threads;++i) {
8    prefix_sum[i]=prefix_sum[i-1]+
         result_sizes[i-1];
9  }
10 //merge local results in parallel
11 for(int i=0;i < num_of_threads;++i) {
12   do parallel: write_thread_result(
         prefix_sum[i],...);
13 }
```

Listing 1.5. Simple parallel scan.

The parallel version of the scan forwards the data array to a number of threads (cf. Listing 1.5, Line 2–4) that build up a local result for the selection on their chunks of the integer array. To allow parallel writing of the local results into a global result without locking, we have to compute the prefix sum (cf. Line 6–9). With this, each thread knows where to copy its local results in the final result array, which is done in parallel (cf. Line 11–13).

3.2   Possible Scan Variants

By combining our four code optimizations, we are able to build a total of 16 variants. The implementation concept of most of the combined variants is straightforward. For instance, adding parallelization to all variants is implemented by changing the work that a single thread is doing. E.g., when combining parallelization and SIMD acceleration, each thread is executing its selection using the SIMD algorithm in Listing 1.4 with some adaptions. Furthermore, implementing branch-free code implies to change the used macro. More challenging is the combination of SIMD and loop unrolling. Here, we took the for-loop (cf. Listing 1.4), put it into another macro and unrolled it for several iterations. To allow reproducibility of our results, we provide our variants as open source implementation.[1]

---

[1] http://wwwiti.cs.uni-magdeburg.de/iti_db/research/gpu/cogadb/supplemental.php.

Table 1. Used evaluation machines.

	Machine 1	Machine 2	Machine 3	Machine 4
CPU	Intel Core 2 Quad Q9550	Intel Core i5-2500	2*Intel Xeon E5-2609 v2	2*Intel Xeon E5-2690
Architecture	Yorkfield	Sandy Bridge	Ivy Bridge - EP	Sandy Bridge - EP
#Sockets	1	1	2	2
#Cores per Socket	4	4	4	8
#Threads per Core	1	1	1	2
CPU Frequency	2.83 GHz	3.3 GHz	2.5 GHz	2.9 GHz
L1-Cache per Core	128 Kb	256 Kb	256 Kb	512 Kb
L2-Cache per CPU	12 Mb	4*256 Kb	4*256 Kb	8*256 Kb
L3-Cache per CPU	—	6 Mb	10 Mb	20 Mb

4   Performance Comparison

For our performance evaluation, we took four different CPUs to test the hardware's impact on the performance of the scan variants. Each machine runs *Ubuntu 10.04.3 LTS 64-bit* as operating system. We compiled our scan variants with the GNU C++ compiler 4.6.4 with the same flags as used by Răducanu et al. [17]. Our workload consists of in-memory columns with integer values internally stored as 32-bit integer arrays containing between 6 million and 60 million values which is about the cardinality of a column of the Lineorder table in the Star Schema Benchmark of scale factors 1–10. Generated values are equally distributed over the range $[0, 999]$. Another parameter is the selectivity factor which we vary in steps of 10 % between 0 % and 100 % to evaluate its impact. The number of used threads for parallelized scans is equal to the number of available threads on each machine. To reach stable results, we repeated each experiment 100 times and applied a gamma-trimming which omits the slowest and fastest 10 results.

CPU Differences. To provide an overview of the characteristics of the CPUs of used machines, we summarize necessary information in Table 1. For our evaluation, we choose two commodity CPUs and two server CPUs. While machine 1 has only the L2 cache as last level cache and a little bit lower clock speed, machine 2 has three cache levels and the highest clock speed. Machine 3 offers four cores on each of the two sockets, but has the lowest clock frequency per CPU. The server CPU in machine 4 with an octa core on each of the two sockets allows to process 32 threads with enabled Hyper-Threading. Thus, machine 4 should have the best parallelization potential. Furthermore, our chosen CPUs have different architectures, where the newest architecture is built in on machine 3, being the Ivy Bridge.

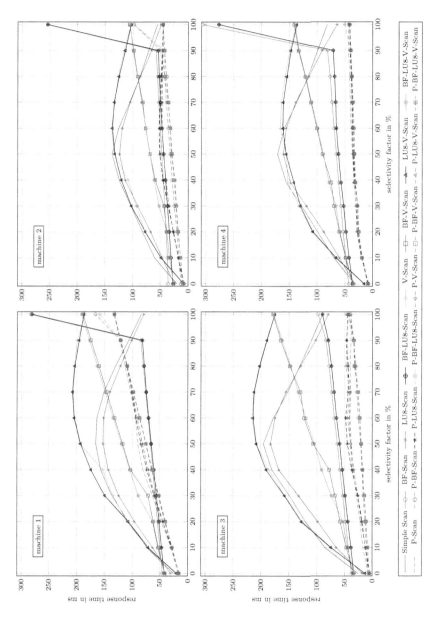

Fig. 1. Response time for 30 million data items (BF = branch-free, LU8 = 8-times loop-unrolled, P = parallelized, V= vectorized).

4.1   Varying Selectivity

In our first experiment, we focus on the performance of our variants for filtering 30 million tuples with different selectivities. For our variants, we implemented a loop unrolling of depth 8 similar to Răducanu et al. [17] and set the number of used threads to the number of available threads on the machine. To produce increasing selectivity factors over our equally distributed values, we evaluate the predicate $x < c$ with increasing comparison constant c. The response times of our 16 algorithms on the four machines are shown in Fig. 1.

From the performance diagrams, we can see that at a selectivity factor smaller than 20%, serial and parallel selections have similar execution times. It is also visible that serial algorithms can outperform parallel algorithms at a selectivity factor of 100%. This performance difference is a result of the overhead produced by the result combination of parallel algorithms which worsens for increasing result sizes.

Furthermore, branching code gets high penalties for medium selectivity factors, making branch-free algorithms superior to them. Nevertheless, the performance of branch-free code is steadily getting worse with increasing selectivity factor till the branching counterpart becomes superior again at a selectivity factor of 100%. Considering unrolling, there are only slight differences between normal loops and unrolled loops. Additionally, the use of SIMD instructions for serial algorithms does not improve the performance as expected. Especially for selectivity factors higher than 50%, the performance of the vectorized scan is almost the worst. This is probably incurred by the expensive mask evaluation which worsens when the selectivity factor increases. However, if we apply loop unrolling and omit branches, we improve the performance significantly, but still, it is not superior to the serial branch-free version.

In summary, a variant that is performing best under all circumstances cannot be found. Although the parallel branch-free loop-unrolled vectorized scan is the best one for machine 3 and 4, it is not for machine 1 at a selectivity factor more than 50%. Here, the serial branch-free scan performs best.

Differences Between Machines. In contrast to the other machines, machine 1 shows that for selectivity factors above 50% the serial branch-free and the serial unrolled branch-free selection execute up to 32% faster than parallel algorithms. Additionally, at a selectivity factor of 100%, even the branching selection and unrolled selection outperform the best parallel algorithm by 39% while the performance of the two branch-free versions deteriorate.

The deterioration of the branch-free serial version for a selectivity factor of 100% is only visible for machine 1, 2, 4. In contrast, machine 3 is not affected, although at this point, the branch-free serial versions are beat by the branching versions. This effect is probably due to the new *next-page prefetcher (NPP)* in the Ivy Bridge architecture in this machine [10]. The NPP prefetches the next cache line if in a sequential access the end of the current cache line is almost reached.

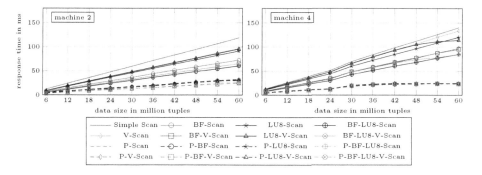

Fig. 2. Response time for different amount of data items for selectivity factor 10 % (BF = branch-free, LU8 = 8-times loop-unrolled, P = parallelized, V= vectorized).

Additionally, while the performance of the branching parallel versions is mostly visibly worse than for the branch-free counterparts (cf. machine 2 & 3), these differences disappear for machine 4. Furthermore, the best performance for serial selections is achieved on machine 2 and for parallel algorithms with machine 4. In addition, on machine 3 & 4 all parallel algorithms perform constantly better than the serial ones.

4.2 Varying Data Size

We analyzed the impact of different data sizes from 6 to 60 million rows for selectivity factors from 0 % to 100 %. Regardless of the selectivity factor, the optimal algorithm does not change with an increasing amount of data. Therefore, we exemplary show our result for selectivity factor 10 % in Fig. 2 for machine 2 and 4.

All variants show increasing response times for increasing data sizes. Furthermore, with increasing data sizes, the performance advantage of parallel algorithms increases compared to serial algorithms. From this, we can conclude that the main impact factor for the optimality of scan-algorithm variants is the selectivity factor; data size has only a minor impact.

Differences Between Machines. Comparing the results from machine 2 with those for machine 4, a big gap between the serial and parallel algorithms is visible on machine 4 that is more severe than on the other machines. The reason for that is that machine 4 has the highest amount of cores and available threads. Thus, machine 4 has the best parallelization capability.

4.3 Different Unrolling Depths

In the overall performance evaluation, we decided to use a common unrolling depth of 8 for the loops [9,17]. However, the number of unrolled executions can be varied, which opens another tuning dimension. In this section, we repeated the evaluation of the serial scan variant and compared it to 2–8 times unrolled serial scans.

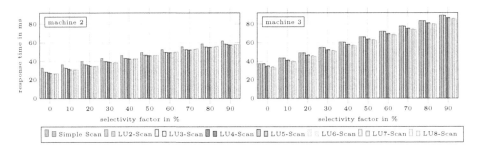

Fig. 3. Response time of branch-free scans with different unrolling depths for varying selectivities for 30 million data items (LUn = n-times loop-unrolled).

Branch-Free Unrolled Scans. The benefit of unrolling depends on the number of executed instructions inside a loop. Thus, we first evaluated the branch-free version of the serial scan for different unrolling depths, because the number of instructions inside the loop does not depend on branching. With this, we assure that we will find the best unrolling depth for a specific machine independent from the selectivity.

In Fig. 3, we visualize the response times for our serial branch-free scans with different unrolling depths on 30 million data items with selectivity factors between 0 % and 90 % for machine 2 and 3. Here, we skipped the selectivity factor 100 %, since the response time behaves the same as for lower selectivity factors, but its overall value is often double as much. Thus, it would deteriorate values in the diagram.

From the performance diagram in Fig. 3, it can be seen that for each machine, there is an optimal unrolling depth. On machine 2, there is in general a huge difference between the serial scan and the unrolled variants. Here, the generally best unrolling depth is five. In contrast, machine 3 benefits from larger unrolling, having its optimum at 8 times unrolling for the considered depths. This circumstance is probably caused by the new Ivy Bridge architecture, because it offers the possibility to combine the micro-op queue of two cores for a single-threaded task in order to process bigger loops more efficiently [10].

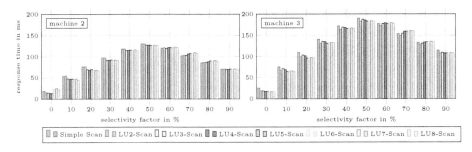

Fig. 4. Response time of branching scans with different unrolling depths for varying selectivities for 30 million data items (LUn = n-times loop-unrolled).

Branching Unrolled Scans. When including branches in our code, the number of executed instructions inside a loop varies depending on the selectivity. Thus, changing behaviors for machine 2 and 3 can be seen in the performance diagrams in Fig. 4. For instance, on machine 2, for selectivity factors from 0 % to 50 % the serial version behaves worse than an unrolling of depth four and for a selectivity factor higher than 50 %, an unrolling of depth three behaves best. Machine 3 shows good performance for 8 times unrolled loops to a selectivity factor of 30 %, where two-times unrolled code gets best till 90 %.

5   Discussion

In the last sections, we presented the evaluation of our scan variants on different machines. We have shown that there are convincing performance differences with respect to varying selectivities and different machines. In this section, we discuss our findings and their impact on a broader view.

5.1   Variant Performance

Our evaluation revealed that there is no optimal scan variant for different CPUs, and for each CPU, it is not trivial to select the optimal variant. Additionally, the optimal variant may change depending on the scan's selectivity.

Branch-Free Code. From the evaluation, we can conclude that performance benefits of branch-free code strongly depends on the selectivity. Nevertheless, we can observe, that branch-free code may degrade performance for the serial or unrolled scan on some machines (cf. Fig. 1; machine 1, 2, 4: selectivity factor 100 %). Instead, for loop unrolling, branch-free code assures that there is an optimal unrolling depth independent of the selectivity.

Loop Unrolling. Loop unrolling offers performance improvements, if (1) the unrolling depth is adjusted to the used processor, and (2) the number of executed instructions in the loop is stable. If the executed instructions in the loop is unstable, the perfect unrolling depth has to be chosen during runtime, for instance, by the hybrid query processing engine HyPE [4]. Nevertheless, loop unrolling does not severely worsen the performance and, thus, it is a valuable optimization that should be considered in every application.

Parallelization. Our results indicate that, in general, parallelization offers a good opportunity for accelerating the scan if the CPU offers enough cores (e.g., on machine 3 or 4). Nevertheless, when parallelized, the scan employs the whole processing capacity of the CPU. With this, response times are maximized, but throughput may be insufficient. Consequently, it has to be carefully weighed whether a parallel scan should be preferred to a serial scan.

Vectorization. Our vectorized scan is most of the times not competitive to other scan variants. However, at low selectivity factors the vectorized scan is the best serial scan, because the probability of excluding several data items in one step is high and beneficial for performance. Its performance loss at higher selectivity factors is caused by the bad result extraction from the bit mask. Hence, instead of expecting a position list as a result, we should rather use a bitmap to represent the result for efficient vectorization.

Concluding, different code optimizations have a varying impact on the performance of a simple scan. Therefore, it is even more challenging to choose an optimal algorithm for more complex operators.

5.2   Threats to Validity

To assure internal validity, we cautiously implemented each variant and equally optimized the code of all variants for performance. We used plain C arrays instead of containers and ensured that the compiler does not perform loop unrolling or auto-vectorization. Our evaluation setup assures that array sizes exceed available cache sizes. Thus, higher sizes should not change the behavior of the variants. However, we executed our tests on machine 3 another time with data sizes of 500 million values without any impact on the general variant performance behaviors.

To reach a high external validity, we extensively show our implementation concepts in Sect. 2, our evaluation environment in Sect. 4 and provide the code to allow for reproducing of our results. However, CoGaDB operates in an operator-at-a-time fashion, which means the whole input is consumed by the operator and the result is then pushed to the next operator. Thus, our results apply to systems that follow this processing paradigm and we expect similar results for vectorized execution.

5.3   Toward Adaptive Variant Selection

As a consequence of the performance differences depending on the used machine and the workload, we need to solve two challenges. First, code optimizations have hardly predictable impacts between machines, which does not allow us to build a simple cost model for an operator. Consequently, we can choose the optimal variant at run-time only by executing and measuring the performance of variants. Second, the number of possible variants is to high to keep them all available during run-time. In fact, for each additional independent optimization, the number of produced variants increases by factor two. Furthermore, possible points where code optimizations make sense will increase with increasing complexity of the optimized operator.

As a solution, we argue to keep a pool of variants for each operator during run-time (cf. Fig. 5). The system generates new variants using optimizations that are likely to be beneficial on the current machine. Variants that perform poor w.r.t. the other variants are deleted and replaced by new variants. As a

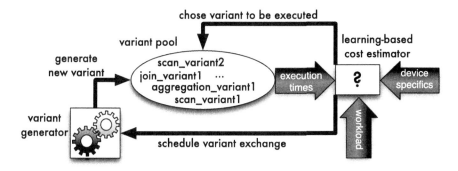

Fig. 5. Adaptive query processing engine

consequence, we also have to think of a suitable approach to generate the variants instead of implementing them by hand.

To select the variant to be executed from the pool, we propose to use a learning-based query execution engine, such as HyPE [4], which learns cost-models for each variant depending on the given machine and workload. With this, we achieve optimized performance due to the usage of best-performing variants from the variant pool for the used machine and also for the current workload. The variant pool itself has to be limited, because learning cost models for many variants introduces too much overhead. Thus, we propose to let the query execution engine decide which algorithm has to be deleted and which one has to be generated, in case it is beneficial for the current or future workload. With this, we achieve a run-time adaptability of our system with respect to the workload and used machine.

Limitations. Our proposed approach relies on good selectivity estimations to choose the optimal variant of the scan and query plan for the given workload. However, we argue that approaches such as kernel-density estimation by Heimel and Markl [8], or work of Markl et al. [14,15] should make it possible to overcome these challenges.

6   Related Work

Răducanu et al. tested different variants of database operations in Vectorwise [17]. Because of the vectorized execution model in Vectorwise, they are able to execute different variants of one database operation during the processing of one column, arguing that different code optimizations are favored by different machines and workloads. Nevertheless, their findings do not reveal the impact of the *combination of code optimizations*, which we expose for the scan operator. In fact, they did not consider different unrolling depths as we do. Furthermore, although we come to the same conclusion as they do, we want to tackle the problem by learning cost models instead of only the execution time of a variant, because we find it more appropriate for our use case.

Related work in the area of code optimizations for stencil computation can be found in the work of Datta et al. [7] and improving scans is topic of the work of Li and Patel [13]. Furthermore, there is much work on applying vectorization on database operations, such as SIMD-accelerated scans for compressed data by Willhalm et al. [19,20], using SIMD instructions for database operations by Zhou and Ross [22], and also using SIMD for accelerating index search by Kim et al. [11] or Zeuch et al. [21]. Their ideas help implementing vectorized database operations, but they compare their implementations only to the serial variant and do not include other code optimizations or machines as we do.

7   Conclusion and Future Work

With the growing heterogeneity of modern processors, it becomes increasingly difficult to exploit their capabilities. Thus, we need an understanding on which hardware characteristics favor which set of code optimizations to achieve the best performance of database operators. Due to interactions between optimizations, this is a non trivial problem.

In this work, we investigated the impact of four different code optimizations and their combinations on the scan operator. We evaluated the performance of the resulting 16 database scan variants on different machines for different workloads. Our results indicate that the performance of most of the algorithms is depending on the selectivity of the scan and also on the used machine. However, when combining code optimizations (e.g. branch-free code and varying loop unrolling depths), simply changing the used machine favors a different algorithm variant. As a consequence, we have to include these variants in the optimization space of our query engine. However, because there are numerous code optimizations and because of their exponential amount of combinations, we run into several problems: building a cost model including each variant is hardly possible, and providing executable code for each variant during run-time is not feasible because of the large number of variants and their respected memory consumption.

Thus, future work includes to learn execution behaviors of the variants by a suitable query engine (e.g., HyPE) that choses the best-performing variant from an algorithm pool and schedules a rejuvenation of the pool which exchanges variants that perform badly for the current workload.

Acknowledgments. We thank Jens Teubner from TU Dortmund and Max Heimel from TU Berlin for helpful feedback and discussions.

References

1. Albutiu, M.C., Kemper, A., Neumann, T.: Massively parallel sort-merge joins in main memory multi-core database systems. PVLDB **5**(10), 1064–1075 (2012)
2. Balkesen, C., Alonso, G., Teubner, J., Özsu, M.T.: Multi-core, main-memory joins: sort vs. hash revisited. PVLDB **7**(1), 85–96 (2013)

3. Balkesen, C., Teubner, J., Alonso, G., Özsu, M.T.: Main-memory hash joins on multi-core CPUs: tuning to the underlying hardware. In: ICDE, pp. 362–373 (2013)
4. Breß, S., Beier, F., Rauhe, H., Sattler, K.U., Schallehn, E., Saake, G.: Efficient co-processor utilization in database query processing. Inf. Sys. **38**(8), 1084–1096 (2013)
5. Breß, S., Siegmund, N., Heimel, M., Saecker, M., Lauer, T., Bellatreche, L., Saake, G.: Load-aware inter-co-processor parallelism in database query processing. Data Knowl. Eng. (2014). doi:10.1016/j.datak.2014.07.003
6. Broneske, D., Breß, S., Heimel, M., Saake, G.: Toward hardware-sensitive database operations. In: EDBT, pp. 229–234 (2014)
7. Datta, K., Murphy, M., Volkov, V., Williams, S., Carter, J., Oliker, L., Patterson, D., Shalf, J., Yelick, K.: Stencil computation optimization and auto-tuning on state-of-the-art multicore architectures. In: SC, pp. 1–12 (2008)
8. Heimel, M., Markl, V.: A first step towards GPU-assisted query optimization. In: ADMS, pp. 33–44 (2012)
9. Hennessy, J.L., Patterson, D.A.: Computer Architecture: A Quantitative Approach, 4th edn. Morgan Kaufmann Publishers Inc, San Francisco (2007)
10. Intel: Intel 64 and IA-32 Architectures Optimization Reference Manual (April 2012). http://www.intel.com/content/dam/doc/manual/64-ia-32-architectures-optimization-manual.pdf
11. Kim, C., Chhugani, J., Satish, N., Sedlar, E., Nguyen, A.D., Kaldewey, T., Lee, V.W., Brandt, S.A., Dubey, P.: FAST: fast architecture sensitive tree search on modern CPUs and GPUs. In: SIGMOD, pp. 339–350 (2010)
12. Leis, V., Boncz, P., Kemper, A., Neumann, T.: Morsel-driven parallelism: a NUMA-aware query evaluation framework for the many-core age. In: SIGMOD, pp. 743–754 (2014)
13. Li, Y., Patel, J.M.: BitWeaving: fast scans for main memory data processing. In: SIGMOD, pp. 289–300 (2013)
14. Markl, V., Lohman, G.M., Raman, V.: LEO: an autonomic query optimizer for DB2. IBM Syst. J. **42**(1), 98–106 (2003)
15. Markl, V., Raman, V., Simmen, D., Lohman, G., Pirahesh, H., Cilimdzic, M.: Robust query processing through progressive optimization. In: SIGMOD, pp. 659–670 (2004)
16. Ross, K.A.: Selection conditions in main-memory. TODS **29**, 132–161 (2004)
17. Răducanu, B., Boncz, P., Zukowski, M.: Micro adaptivity in vectorwise. In: SIGMOD, pp. 1231–1242 (2013)
18. Teubner, J., Mueller, R., Alonso, G.: Frequent item computation on a chip. TDKE **23**(8), 1169–1181 (2011)
19. Willhalm, T., Boshmaf, Y., Plattner, H., Popovici, N., Zeier, A., Schaffner, J.: SIMD-Scan: ultra fast in-memory table scan using on-chip vector processing units. PVLDB **2**(1), 385–394 (2009)
20. Willhalm, T., Oukid, I., Müller, I., Faerber, F.: Vectorizing database column scans with complex predicates. In: ADMS, pp. 1–12 (2013)
21. Zeuch, S., Freytag, J.C., Huber, F.: Adapting tree structures for processing with SIMD instructions. In: EDBT, pp. 97–108 (2014)
22. Zhou, J., Ross, K.A.: Implementing database operations using SIMD instructions. In: SIGMOD, pp. 145–156 (2002)

Efficient Transaction Processing for Hyrise in Mixed Workload Environments

David Schwalb[1(✉)], Martin Faust[1], Johannes Wust[1], Martin Grund[2], and Hasso Plattner[1]

[1] Hasso Plattner Institute, Potsdam, Germany
david.schwalb@hpi.de
[2] eXascale Infolab, University of Fribourg, Fribourg, Switzerland

Abstract. Hyrise is an in-memory storage engine designed for mixed enterprise workloads that originally started as a research prototype for hybrid table layouts and basic transaction processing capabilities. This paper presents our incremental improvements and learnings to better support transactional consistency in mixed workloads.

In particular, the paper addresses a multi-version concurrency control mechanism with lock-free commit steps, tree-based multi-column indices, in-memory optimized logging and recovery mechanisms. Additionally, a mixed workload scheduling mechanism is presented, addressing partitionable transactional workloads in combination with analytical queries.

1 Introduction

Currently, we are observing three different trends in the database community. First, traditional general purpose database systems are evolving and incorporate new technologies [2,12,19]. Second, the separation between transactional processing (OLTP) and analytical processing (OLAP) systems continues. Extremely specialized systems leverage the partition-ability of some transactional workloads and completely serialize the execution on partitions to eliminate the overhead of concurrency control [7,17,23]. However, support for cross-partition queries or analytical queries is poor [24]. Third and in contrast to second, we see a unification of both system types, taking on the challenge of executing a mixed workload of transactional and analytical queries in one system [5,9,15,16,18,20,21]. This unification is based on the characteristics of enterprise databases and builds on the set-based processing of typical business economics applications and the low number of updates allowing an insert only approach. The unification provides real time insights on the transactional data and eliminates redundancies.

The in-memory storage engine Hyrise targets a unified transactional and analytical system and is designed to support vertical partitioning of tables to allow for the optimal storage layout for mixed enterprise workloads [5]. It builds on a main-delta-concept leveraging light-weight compression techniques like dictionary encoding and bit-packing. It supports an efficient merge process [10] as well as a balanced execution of mixed enterprise workloads [27].

© Springer International Publishing Switzerland 2015
A. Jagatheesan et al. (Eds.): IMDM 2013/2014, LNCS 8921, pp. 112–125, 2015.
DOI: 10.1007/978-3-319-13960-9_9

Contribution. In this paper, we provide an overview of implementation aspects of Hyrise and describe optimizations to better support transactional workloads. In particular, we describe (a) a multi-version concurrency control mechanism with a lock-free commit step in Sect. 3, (b) a tree-based multi-column index structure in Sect. 4, (c) a persistency mechanism optimized for in-memory data-bases and parallel recovery in Sect. 5 and (d) an optimized scheduling mechanism for the scheduling of mixed workloads while still leveraging the partition-ability of transactional workloads in Sect. 6.

2 Architecture

Hyrise is an in-memory storage engine[1] specifically targeted to mixed workload scenarios [5] and the balanced execution of both analytical and transactional workloads at the same time [27]. In this section, we describe the basic architecture of the system.

Although Hyrise supports flexible hybrid storage layouts, we assume a colum-nar storage of tables. The table data consists of attribute vectors and dictionar-ies for each column in the table as well as three additional columns used for concurrency control. Hyrise uses multi-version concurrency control to manage transactions, providing snapshot isolation as a default isolation level and allow-ing for higher isolation levels on request, as described in more detail in Sect. 3. Additionally, the transaction manager handles a transaction context for each running transaction.

Based on analyses of workloads of productive enterprise applications, Hyrise is optimized for read-only queries in order to optimally support the dominant query types based on the set processing nature of business applications [10]. Data modifications follow the insert-only approach and updates are always modeled as new inserts and deletes. Deletes only invalidate rows. We keep the insertion order of tuples and only the lastly inserted version is valid. The insert-only approach in combination with multi-versioning allows Hryise to process writers without stalling readers. Additionally, keeping the history of tables provides the ability of time-travel queries [8] or to keep the full history due to legal requirements [18]. Furthermore, tables are always stored physically as collections of attributes and meta-data and each attribute consists of two partitions: main and delta partition.

The main partition is typically dictionary compressed using an ordered dic-tionary, replacing values in the tuples with encoded values from the dictionary. In order to minimize the overhead of maintaining the sort order, incoming updates are accumulated in the write-optimized delta partition as described in [10,22]. In contrast to the main partition, data in the write-optimized delta partition is stored using an unsorted dictionary. In addition, a tree-based index with all the unique uncompressed values of the delta partition is maintained per column. The index on top of the dictionary allows for fast value searches on the dictionary and also speeds up value insert into the column, as inserting a value into a dictionary encoded column requires to search the dictionary [20]. The attribute vectors of

---

[1] Source code available at https://github.com/hyrise/hyrise.

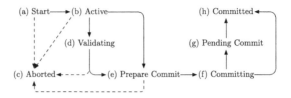

Fig. 1. Internal Hyrise transaction states. Once a transaction entered phase (f) no more logical transaction aborts are possible. Validation phase (d) is optional depending on additional validation steps for serializability.

both partitions, storing the dictionary encoded values, are further compressed using bit-packing mechanisms [3,25].

To ensure a constantly small size of the delta partition, Hyrise executes a periodic merge process. A merge process combines all data from the main partition as well as the delta partition to create a new main partition that then serves as the primary data store [10].

3   Concurrency Control

The choice between an optimistic or pessimistic concurrency control approach highly depends on the expected workload [1,11]. Hyrise uses a multi-version concurrency control (MVCC) mechanism to provide snapshot isolation. This optimistic approach fits well with the targeted mixed workload enterprise environment, as the number of expected conflicts is low and long running analytical queries can run on a consistent snapshot of the database [18]. This section describes our concurrency control implementation that is based on known MVCC mechanisms and focuses on the parallel commit of transactions.

In Hyrise, the transaction manager is responsible for tracking a monotonically increasing next transaction id $ntid$ and the last visible commit id $lcid$, as well as maintaining a commit context list ccl. Each transaction keeps local information in a *transaction context* containing a local last visible commit id $lcid_T$, its own transaction id tid_T and two lists referencing inserted and deleted rows plus a reference to a commit context in case the transaction is in the commit phase. Each table maintains three additional vectors: a transaction id vector $vtid$ used to lock rows for deletion and two commit id vectors $vbeg$ and $vend$ indicating the validity of rows.

Transactions can be in 8 different phases: (a) transaction start, (b) active processing, (c) transaction aborted, (d) validating, (e) preparing commit, (f) transaction committing, (g) pending commit and (h) transaction committed. Figure 1 shows the actual states and how transactions can change between them.

3.1   Start Transaction Phase

When a new transaction is started, it enters the start phase and is assigned a unique transaction id tid_T by the transaction manager. Additionally, the transaction copies the global last visible transaction id $lcid$ to the local transaction

Table 1. Evaluation rules determining the visibility of rows for a transaction T. Not yet committed inserts and deletes are listed as 'dirty'. *Impossible combination as rows are always activated before they are invalidated.

	Own? $vtid = tid_T$	Activated? $vbeg \leq lcid_T$	Invalidated? $vend \leq lcid_T$	Row visible?
Past Delete	yes	yes	yes	no
Past Delete	no	yes	yes	no
Impossible*	yes	no	yes	no
Dirty Own Delete	yes	yes	no	no
Impossible*	no	no	yes	no
Own Insert	yes	no	no	yes
Past Insert/Future delete	no	yes	no	yes
Dirty Insert/Future Insert	no	no	no	no

context as $lcid_T$. After the transaction context is successfully prepared, the transaction enters the active state. During processing and validation, write-write conflicts might occur leaving the transaction in the aborted state. Once a transaction enters the commit phase, the transaction is guaranteed to commit successfully and to reach the committed state.

3.2 Active Processing Phase

During active processing, a transaction T might read or write rows and needs to guarantee the required isolation level. Whenever a set of rows is retrieved from a table through either a table scan operation or an index lookup, the set of rows is validated based on the respective $vbeg$, $vend$ and $vtid$ values of a row in combination with $lcid_T$ and tid_T. Table 1 outlines the different combinations and if T sees them as visible. Some combinations are impossible based on the design of the commit mechanism but listed for completeness. Not yet committed inserts and deletes are listed as dirty. In case transactions need a higher isolation level, serializability can be requested to enforce read stability and phantom avoidance through additional checks before the commit step [11].

Inserts are straight forward, appending a new row to the delta partition of a table with $vtid = tid_T$. As $vbeg$ and $vend$ are initialized to ∞, the new row is only visible to T and no other transaction can read the in-flight row before T successfully commits. Deletes only invalidate rows by setting $vend$. However, as a transaction does not have a commit id in the active phase, it only deletes the row locally in the transaction context and marking the row by setting $vtid$ to tid_T with an atomic compare-and-swap operation. This blocks any subsequent transaction from deleting the same row, resulting in the detection of write-write conflicts. Updates are realized as an insert of the new version with an invalidation of the old version.

Algorithm 3.1. FINISHCOMMIT(c)

$c.pending \leftarrow True$
while c **and** $c.pending$
$$\text{do} \begin{cases} \textbf{if } atomic\_cas(lcid, c.cid - 1, c.cid) \begin{cases} send\_response(c) \\ c \leftarrow c.next \end{cases} \\ \textbf{else } \{\textbf{return } (0) \end{cases}$$

3.3   Lock-Free Commit Phase

Multiple transactions can enter the commit phase in parallel and synchronization is handled by the following lock-free mechanism. Although transactions can process their commit step in parallel, cascading commits realized by using commit dependencies guarantee the correct ordering of the final step of incrementing $lcid$.

Once a transaction T is ready to commit, it enters the prepare commit phase and is assigned a commit context c. Through an atomic insertion of c into the global commit context list ccl, a unique commit id cid_T is implicitly assigned to the committing transaction by incrementing the id of the predecessor. Each commit context contains the transaction's commit id cid_T, connection information to send a response to the client and a next pointer to the next commit context in the list. The insertion into ccl is performed by executing a compare and swap operation on the next pointer of the last commit context lcx to c. Although this mechanism is not wait-free, it provides a lock-free way of creating a linked list of commit contexts with sequentially increasing commit ids. T is guaranteed to proceed to the actual commit phase after successfully inserting c and can not enter the abort state anymore. During the commit phase, T traverses all its changes by iterating through the list of inserted and deleted rows and writing the commit id. Inserted rows are committed by setting $vbeg$ to cid_T and all deleted rows are committed by setting $vend$ to cid_T.

Finally, T determines if it can directly enter the committed state or if it needs to enter the pending commit state. As multiple transactions can enter the commit phase concurrently, it is possible that transactions T_1 and T_2 commit concurrently and $cid_{T2} > cid_{T1}$. If T_2 enters the committed state first, it would set the global $lcid$ to cid_{T2}. However, due to the implemented visibility mechanism through one single last visible commit id, this would allow newly starting transaction to see the in-flight changes of T_1, which is still not fully committed. A pessimistic approach might serialize the commit phases of transactions and avoid this problem. However, if a large number of rows is touched leading to longer commit phases, this quickly turns into a bottleneck. Therefore, Hyrise supports parallel commits that allow transactions to commit in any order except for the last step of incrementing the global $lcid$. Instead, commit dependencies take care of incrementing $lcid$ at the correct point in time and only then the respective transactions are returned as committed to the client. This allows parallel and lock-free commit phases and although the final commit step might be deferred, worker threads are already freed and can process other queries.

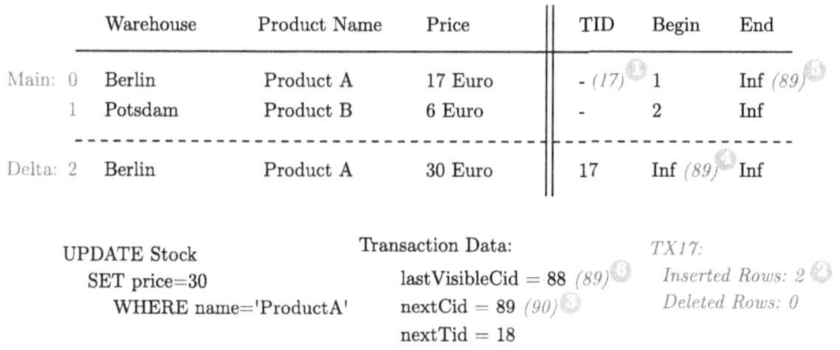

	Warehouse	Product Name	Price	TID	Begin	End
Main: 0	Berlin	Product A	17 Euro	- (17)	1	Inf (89)
1	Potsdam	Product B	6 Euro	-	2	Inf
Delta: 2	Berlin	Product A	30 Euro	17	Inf (89)	Inf

UPDATE Stock
SET price=30
WHERE name='ProductA'

Transaction Data:
lastVisibleCid = 88 *(89)*
nextCid = 89 *(90)*
nextTid = 18

TX17:
Inserted Rows: 2
Deleted Rows: 0

Fig. 2. Example outlining the implemented multi-version concurrency algorithm.

Algorithm 3.1 outlines the process of the final commit step that allows workers to finish processing of a transaction by adding a commit dependency although the final last step of incrementing $lcid$ might not yet be possible. First, a committing transaction T_1 with commit context c sets its commit context status to pending and indicates that it is trying to increment the $lcid$. Then, T_1 tries to atomically increment the $lcid$. In case the increment failed, T_1 depends on another currently committing transaction T_2 with $cid_{T2} < cid_{T1}$ to commit T_1. The processing worker thread is then freed and can process new queries. The atomic incrementation of $lcid$ ensures that only one thread succeeds even if multiple threads are concurrently incrementing $lcid$. When T_2 finally commits, it checks if pending transactions exist by following the list of commit contexts. As long as there are pending commits, T_2 proceeds and increments the $lcid$.

The fact that the $lcid$ is only updated after all commit ids for $vbeg$ and $vend$ have been written, ensures that all changes during the commit phase appear to other transactions as future operations, leaving the affected records untouched from the viewpoint of other transactions. Until the global $lcid$ is set to cid_T of a committing transaction and makes all changes visible for subsequent transactions in one atomic step.

3.4   Aborts

Transactions can only abort before they enter the commit phase. Therefore, aborting transactions do not yet have an assigned commit id and have only inserted new rows which are still invisible or have marked a row locally for deletion. This means that an aborting transaction only has to clear potentially locked rows by removing their id from $vtid$ using the lists of inserted and deleted rows from the transaction context.

3.5   Example

Figure 2 shows an example of an update query with $tid_T = 17$ setting the price of a product A from 17 to 30. The image shows a logical view of a table separated into main and delta partitions. (1) Row 0 is locked by setting $vtid = 17$, (2) the new version of the row is inserted into the delta and added to the local list of inserted rows, (3) the commit phase starts, assigning T the commit id $cid_T = 89$, (4) $vbeg$ of the newly inserted row is set to 89 though it is still invisible to other running transactions as the $lcid$ is still 88, (5) the old row gets invalidated by setting $vend = 89$ and added to the local list of deleted rows, (6) the $lcid$ gets incremented making all changes visible to other transactions.

4   Index Structures

Hyrise allows the definition of indices to efficiently support transactional queries which select only a few tuples. Index data structures are maintained separately for the main and delta partition of columns to account for their different characteristics. The following describes a read-only Group-Key Index for the main partition of a single column [4], a tree-based index structure for the delta partition and index structures on multiple columns.

4.1   Single Column Indices

A single-column index on the main partition leverages the read-only nature of the main partition to reduce the storage footprint by creating an immutable structure for the mapping of values to positions during the merge process. The main index consists of two bit-packed vectors that map dictionary entries to position lists.

It consists of an offset vector O and a position vector P. O is parallel to the dictionary D of a column and contains the start of the list of values in P for each value in D, in other words the offset which is used to jump into P. P is parallel to the attribute vector AV and contains all row positions sorted by their value. Thereby all rows for a distinct value can be retrieved with only two direct reads at the respective position in the two vectors O and P.

In contrast to the main index, the delta index needs to efficiently handle newly inserted values and is implemented as a multi-map of actual values and positions using a tree-based data structure. Entries are kept in ascending order so that the list of positions for a single value is always sorted. Figure 3(b) shows a schematic overview of the used index structures.

4.2   Multi Column Indices

Hyrise supports the indexing of multiple columns through the usage of *Composite Group-Keys* on the main partition and tuple-indexing on the delta partition. The challenge for our column-oriented in-memory store is to efficiently obtain a unique identifier from the composite key, as the parts of the key are encoded and not co-located. In Hyrise, Composite Group-Key Indices store the concatenation of a key's value- ids in a key-identifier list K, as shown in Fig. 3(a).

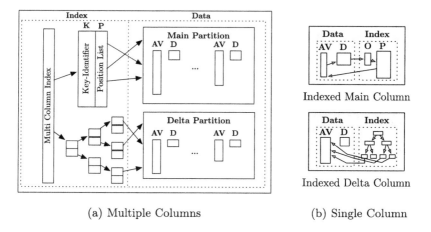

(a) Multiple Columns   (b) Single Column

Fig. 3. Overview of index data structures on single columns and multiple columns for main and delta partitions. Main: Value lookup in dictionary D, jumping from offset vector O into positions vector P, referencing values in attribute vector AV. Delta: Tree-based index on values referencing attribute vector.

This leads to an additional dictionary lookup for each part of the key before the index lookup, since all values of the predicate have to be transformed into value-ids prior to a binary search on K. The offset of the found key-identifier can be used to directly obtain the row-id from the position list P. In the delta partition, where the storage footprint is not as important as in the main partition, we concatenate the actual values in the index. We use transformations similar to Leis et al. [13] to obtain binary-comparable keys.

Internally, Hyrise uses different strongly-typed data types. To allow the flexible definition and querying of multi-column indices at runtime, the system provides key-builder objects that accept any internal data type. Multiple calls to a key builder object can be executed with different data types, which allows to conveniently and efficiently support composite keys with mixed data types.

Indices are unaware of the visibility of records. Hence, the delta index is used in an append-only manner and retrieved records need to be validated using the defined visibility mechanism. In case of primary key lookups, the index is traversed backwards to find the first valid version of a key. While this increases the lookup overhead moderately, it allows to maintain the visibility information at one single location and to have transaction-agnostic index structures.

5 Persistency: Logging, Recovery and Checkpointing

Although in-memory databases keep their primary copy of the data in main memory, they still require logging mechanisms to achieve durability. The persistency mechanisms applied in Hyrise differ from traditional disk-based mechanisms due to the lack of a paging mechanism and the used multi-version concurrency control. In this section, we describe the implemented logging, checkpointing and recovery mechanisms.

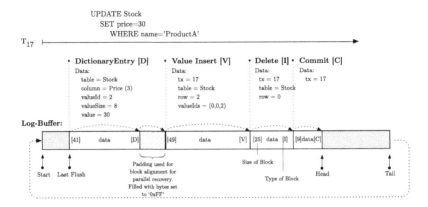

Fig. 4. Delta Log Format. Last flush marks entries already flushed to disk. Padding is used to align log-file for parallel recovery, log entries are fixed sized based on their type, only dictionary entries have a variable length.

The main partition of a table is always stored as a binary dump on disk after a merge process. Therefore, only changes to the delta are written to a log file, which uses group commits to hide the latency of disks or SSDs. Checkpoints create a consistent snapshot of the database by also dumping the delta partitions as binary dumps. In a recovery case, existing dumps for main and delta are restored from a checkpoint and an eventually existing delta log is replayed to restore the latest consistent state of tables. Binary dumps are a snapshot of a table persisted onto disk in the form of binary files directly storing the respective data structures. Separate files for the table meta-data containing the number and name of columns, attribute vectors, dictionaries and indexes are created. Using this information, the system is able to recreate the complete table by loading the respective files.

5.1 Delta Log

In contrast to ARIES style logging techniques [14], logging in Hyrise leverages the applied dictionary compression [26] and only writes redo information to the log. This to reduce the overall log size by writing dictionary-compressed values and parallel recovery as log entries can be replayed in any order.

The actual log entries that are written to the log-file are of the following 8 types: (1) dictionary entries indicate a newly inserted value with its value id, (2) value entries indicate a newly inserted row in a table, (3) invalidations invalidate an existing row, (4) commit entries indicate a successfully committed transaction, (5) rollback entries indicate that a transaction performed a rollback and aborted, (6) skip entries are padding entries used for alignment, (7) checkpoint start entries indicate the start of a checkpoint, (8) checkpoint end entries indicate the end of a checkpoint. Dictionary Entries do not include the inserting transaction's TID, as this information is irrelevant to the recovery process. Even if a transaction that inserted a value into the dictionary needs to be rolled back, the value can stay in the dictionary without compromising functionality. If a log entry is to be written and its size would overlap into another block, the remaining space is filled with a Skip Entry and the log entry is written to the beginning of the next block in order to align the log-file to a specified block-size. Thereby, it is guaranteed that log entries to not span across block boundaries which allows easy parallel recovery as thread can start reading the log entries at block boundaries. Skip entries consist only out of bytes set to $0xFF$ and introduce only a minimal overhead as block sizes for the alignment are typically in the range of multiple megabytes.

Figure 4 outlines the used format for writing the log file. New log entries are buffered in a ring-buffer before they are flushed to the log-file. Similarly to recent work, buffer fill operations are only synchronized while acquiring buffer regions and threads can fill their regions in parallel [6]. Each entry in the buffer starts with a character specifying the size of the entry, followed by its data and closed by the type of the entry. This design allows to forward iterate through the list of entries by skipping the respective sizes of entries and to read the log entries backwards in case of recovery by processing each entry based on its type. Entries do have a fixed length based on their type, except variable length dictionary entries which contain a dedicated value length in the log entry.

5.2   Checkpointing

Checkpoints create a consistent snapshot of the database as a binary dump on disk in order to speed up recovery. They are periodically initiated by a checkpoint daemon running in the background. In a recovery case, only the binary dumps from the last checkpoint need to be loaded and only the part starting at the last checkpoint time from the delta log needs to be replayed. In contrast to disk based database systems where a buffer manager only needs to flush all dirty pages in order to create a snapshot, Hyrise needs to persist the complete delta partition of all tables including $vbeg$ and $vend$.

A checkpoint is created in three steps: (1) prepare checkpoint, (2) write checkpoint and (3) finish checkpoint. In the first step, the checkpoint is assigned a unique id and the global log file is switched from the current file A to a new empty log file B, redirecting all subsequent log entries into the new file. The first entry in the new log file is the checkpoint start entry. Additionally, the necessary folder structure is created with a file indicating that the checkpoint is in progress. The transaction manager then waits for all currently running transactions to finish before the checkpoint enters the next phase. This guarantees that log file B contains all relevant information to roll forward to the latest consistent state during recovery. This mechanism adds a delay to the checkpoint process, but does not block any transactions from executing. In the second phase, the actual checkpoint is written and all delta tables are written in a binary format to disk, including eventually existing index structures. Additionally, the $vbeg$ and $vend$ of all tables are persisted to disk, as the delta potentially contains updated versions of rows from the main. In the third and final checkpoint phase, a checkpoint end entry is written to the log and a file is created indicating that the checkpoint as

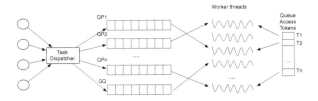

Fig. 5. Task queues for partitionable transactions

finished successfully. This makes the checkpoint the latest available checkpoint in the system so that it will be used in case of a recovery. Due to the applied insert only approach, the checkpoint mechanism can operate concurrently as writing transactions are executed.

5.3   Recovery Process

The recovery process is executed in two steps: (1) load checkpoint and (2) replay delta log. The checkpoint contains binary dumps of the main and delta partition and is loaded in parallel. The delta replay step can be easily distributed across multiple threads based on the layout of the log-file in blocks.

Each thread reads its assigned blocks from the back and replays all successfully committed transactions which are identified by a commit entry as their first log entry. This can be executed in parallel without any synchronization as the log entry replay is independent of the replay order. The only requirement is some upfront meta-data about table sizes, dictionary sizes and transaction numbers in order to preallocate the data structures. In case a thread does not read a commit entry for one transaction, it needs to make sure that no other thread has processed the respective commit entry before ultimately discarding the changes of this transaction. This synchronization between threads is handled by setting a field in a global bit- vector based on the transaction id for each processed commit entry and parking all log entries that are not preceded by a commit entry for later evaluation. After the processing of all blocks, the threads are synchronized through a barrier and reevaluate all discarded transactions by checking if another thread read a commit entry by looking up the transaction id in the bit-vector and replaying the changes if necessary.

Both steps are reasonably optimized and implemented distributing the work across all available cores to fully leverage the available parallelism and bandwidth on modern systems to provide the fastest possible delta log replay.

6   Scheduling

To execute mixed database workloads, Hyrise leverages a task-based query execution model. The main advantages of this execution model are (1) almost perfect load balancing on multi-core CPUs, (2) efficient workload management based on a non-preemptive priority task scheduling policy.

The general idea of this execution model is to partition a query into smaller, non-preemptive units of work, so called tasks, and map these tasks dynamically to a pool of worker threads by a user-level scheduler. Short running OLTP queries are executed as a single task, complex OLAP style queries are transformed into a graph of fine granular tasks by applying data parallelism on operator level. The granularity of tasks is controlled by a system parameter for the maximum task size. Each partitionable operator is split dynamically at runtime into tasks, based on the size of the input data and the maximum task size [27].

The task-based execution model achieves almost perfect load balancing, as the actual degree of parallelism for executing complex queries can vary dynamically throughout execution depending on the current workload. Assuming a complex query is executed as the only query on a multi-core machine, it can leverage all worker threads for execution. Once another query enters the system, tasks of both queries are distributed over the available worker threads taking query priorities or predefined resource shares into account [28,29].

To optimize scheduling for transactional throughput, we extend the task-based execution model by introducing specific queues for partitionable transactions. Note that we still apply the concurrency control mechanism described in Sect. 3 to enable transaction safe read access for analytical queries based on snapshot isolation. Figure 5 gives an overview of the concept of transaction specific queues. Queries that modify data of a particular data partition n are placed in one of the corresponding queues shown as QPn in Fig. 5. Analytical queries are placed in the general queue GQ. Each worker thread tries to pull tasks from the partitionable queues with priority and only takes tasks from the general queue, if no tasks from transactional query is available. Tasks of one partition are serialized through a token mechanism to ensure that only one transactional query per partition is executed at a time. This mechanism avoids the execution of multiple tasks of one partition and therefore eliminates possible write conflicts.

7 Conclusion

In this paper, we presented implementation specific design choices for the in-memory storage engine Hyrise to optimize transaction processing in a mixed enterprise workload setting. We outlined the main architectural design choices and addressed the following parts in particular: (1) a multi-version concurrency control mechanism with lock-free commit steps, (2) tree-based multi-column indices, (3) in-memory optimized logging and recovery mechanisms and (4) a mixed workload scheduling mechanism addressing partition-able transactional workloads in combination with analytical queries.

References

1. Bernstein, P.A., Hadzilacos, V., Goodman, N.: Concurrency Control and Recovery in Database Systems. Addison-Wesley, Reading (1987)
2. Diaconu, C., Freedman, C., Ismert, E., Larson, P.-A., Mittal, P., Stonecipher, R., Verma, N., Zwilling, M.: Hekaton: SQL server's memory-optimized OLTP engine. In: SIGMOD (2013)

3. Faust, M., Grund, M., Berning, T., Schwalb, D., Plattner, H.: Vertical bit-packing: optimizing operations on bit-packed vectors leveraging SIMD instructions. In: Han, W.-S., Lee, M.L., Muliantara, A., Sanjaya, N.A., Thalheim, B., Zhou, S. (eds.) DASFAA 2014. LNCS, vol. 8505, pp. 132–145. Springer, Heidelberg (2014)

4. Faust, M., Schwalb, D., Krueger, J., Plattner, H.: Fast lookups for in-memory column stores: group-key indices, lookup and maintenance. In: ADMS in Conjunction with VLDB (2012)

5. Grund, M., Krueger, J., Plattner, H., Zeier, A., Cudre-Mauroux, P., Madden, S.: HYRISE–a main memory hybrid storage engine. In: VLDB (2010)

6. Johnson, R., Pandis, I., Stoica, R., Athanassoulis, M., Ailamaki, A.: Aether: a scalable approach to logging. In: VLDB (2010)

7. Kallman, R., Kimura, H., Natkins, J., Pavlo, A., Rasin, A., Zdonik, S., Jones, E., Madden, S., Stonebraker, M., Zhang, Y.: H-store: a high-performance, distributed main memory transaction processing system. In: VLDB (2008)

8. Kaufmann, M., Vagenas, P., Fischer, P.M., Kossmann, D., Färber, F.: Comprehensive and interactive temporal query processing with SAP HANA. In: VLDB (2013)

9. Kemper, A., Neumann, T.: HyPer: a hybrid OLTP&OLAP main memory database system based on virtual memory snapshots. In: ICDE (2011)

10. Krüger, J., Kim, C., Grund, M., Satish, N., Schwalb, D., Chhugani, J., Plattner, H., Dubey, P., Zeier, A.: Fast updates on read-optimized databases using multi-core CPUs. In: VLDB (2011)

11. Larson, P.-A., Blanas, S., Diaconu, C., Freedman, C., Patel, J.M., Zwilling, M.: High-performance concurrency control mechanisms for main-memory databases. In: VLDB (2011)

12. Larson, P.-A., Clinciu, C., Hanson, E.N., Oks, A., Price, S.L., Rangarajan, S., Surna, A., Zhou, Q.: SQL server column store indexes. In: SIGMOD (2011)

13. Leis, V., Kemper, A., Neumann, T.: The adaptive radix tree: ARTful indexing for main-memory databases. In: ICDE (2013)

14. Mohan, C., Haderle, D., Lindsay, B., Pirahesh, H., Schwarz, P.: ARIES: a transaction recovery method supporting fine-granularity locking and partial rollbacks using write-ahead logging. In: TODS (1998)

15. Mühe, H., Kemper, A., Neumann, T.: Executing long-running transactions in synchronization-free main memory database systems. In: CIDR (2013)

16. Mühlbauer, T., Rödiger, W., Reiser, A., Kemper, A., Neumann, T.: ScyPer: a hybrid OLTP&OLAP distributed main memory database system for scalable real-time analytics. In: BTW (2013)

17. Pandis, I., Johnson, R., Hardavellas, N., Ailamaki, A.: Data-oriented transaction execution. In: VLDB (2010)

18. Plattner, H.: A common database approach for OLTP and OLAP using an in-memory column database. In: SIGMOD (2009)

19. Raman, V., Attaluri, G., Barber, R., Chainani, N., Kalmuk, D., KulandaiSamy, V., Leenstra, J., Lightstone, S., Liu, S., Lohman, G.M., Malkemus, T., Mueller, R., Pandis, I., Schiefer, B., Sharpe, D., Sidle, R., Storm, A., Zhang, L.: DB2 with BLU acceleration: so much more than just a column store. In: VLDB (2013)

20. Schwalb, D., Faust, M., Krueger, J., Plattner, H.: Physical column organization in in-memory column stores. In: Meng, W., Feng, L., Bressan, S., Winiwarter, W., Song, W. (eds.) DASFAA 2013, Part II. LNCS, vol. 7826, pp. 48–63. Springer, Heidelberg (2013)

21. Sikka, V., Färber, F., Lehner, W., Cha, S.K., Peh, T., Bornhövd, C.: Efficient transaction processing in SAP HANA database - the end of a column store myth. In: SIGMOD (2012)
22. Stonebraker, M., Abadi, D., Batkin, A., Chen, X., Cherniack, M., Ferreira, M., Lau, E., Lin, A., Madden, S., O'Neil, E.: C-store: a column-oriented DBMS. In: VLDB (2005)
23. Stonebraker, M., Weisberg, A.: The VoltDB main memory DBMS. IEEE Data Eng. Bull. **36**(2), 21–27 (2013)
24. Tu, S., Zheng, W., Kohler, E., Liskov, B., Madden, S.: Speedy transactions in multicore in-memory databases. In: SOSP (2013)
25. Willhalm, T., Popovici, N., Boshmaf, Y., Plattner, H., Zeier, A., Schaffner, J.: SIMD-Scan: ultra fast in-memory table scan using on-chip vector processing units. In: VLDB (2009)
26. Wust, J., Boese, J.-H., Renkes, F., Blessing, S., Krueger, J., Plattner, H.: Efficient logging for enterprise workloads on column-oriented in-memory databases. In: CIKM (2012)
27. Wust, J., Grund, M., Hoewelmeyer, K., Schwalb, D., Plattner, H.: Concurrent execution of mixed enterprise workloads on in-memory databases. In: Bhowmick, S.S., Dyreson, C.E., Jensen, C.S., Lee, M.L., Muliantara, A., Thalheim, B. (eds.) DASFAA 2014, Part I. LNCS, vol. 8421, pp. 126–140. Springer, Heidelberg (2014)
28. Wust, J., Grund, M., Plattner, H.: Dynamic query prioritization for in-memory databases. In: IMDM in Conjunction with VLDB (2013)
29. Wust, J., Grund, M., Plattner, H.: Tamex: a task-based query execution framework for mixed enterprise workloads on in-memory databases. In: GI-Jahrestagung (2013)

The DCB-Tree: A Space-Efficient Delta Coded Cache Conscious B-Tree

Robert Binna[✉], Dominic Pacher, Thomas Meindl, and Günther Specht

Databases and Information Systems, Institute of Computer Science,
University of Innsbruck, Innsbruck, Austria
{robert.binna,dominic.pacher,thomas.meindl,gunther.specht}@uibk.ac.at

Abstract. Main-memory index structures have become mainstream for
a large number of problem domains. However, in the case of web-based
datasets, which feature exponential growth, it is an ongoing challenge
to fit those data entirely in main-memory. In this paper, we present
the DCB-Tree, an extremely space efficient main-memory index structure
for the storage of short fixed-size keys. It features a two-stage cache-line
aligned node layout. In comparison to other main-memory index structures it reduces the amount of memory required by 80 % in the best and
by 30 % in the worst case. Although it is tailored towards space consumption, it features good overall performance characteristics. In particular,
in the case of very large real world datasets it provides performance equal
or superior to state of the art main-memory index structures.

Keywords: Indexing · Main-memory · Delta-encoding · Cache-optimized

1 Introduction

With the amount of main-memory capacities increasing, many databases can be
kept entirely in main-memory. However, this is not the case for all domains. For
example, the exponential growth of web-based datasets results in huge semantic
web data or full-text corpuses. Although data can be sharded and distributed
onto several hosts, it is still desirable to reduce the amount of memory needed
and therefore to reduce the monetary cost as well. In the case of RDF-Stores
[5,18] a common approach to reduce the amount of memory needed for indexing
such kind of data, is to solely store fixed size keys instead of long variable length
values and place the original value in a dictionary. Hence to reduce the amount
of memory required, the dictionary or the fixed length keys can be compressed.

As the main purpose of index structures is to improve the search and query
performance, the space consumption of such indexes is a trade-off between access
performance and compression ratio. Nevertheless, the compression overhead can
be mitigated due to the memory wall effect [22], which states that the improvement in microprocessor speed exceeds the improvement in DRAM performance.
Currently DRAM speed is more than two orders of magnitude slower than CPU
speed. This situation is comparable to the performance disparity between main-
memory and disks. As disk based index structures use compression techniques

© Springer International Publishing Switzerland 2015
A. Jagatheesan et al. (Eds.): IMDM 2013/2014, LNCS 8921, pp. 126–138, 2015.
DOI: 10.1007/978-3-319-13960-9_10

to reduce the required number of disk seeks [8]. According to the famous quote "memory is the new disk" [10] it can be inferred that "cache is the new RAM". Hence, compressing data on a cache-line level can trade instructions required for compression against CPU cycles gained by reducing the number of cache misses. The memory wall effect becomes even more significant for index structures consisting of several 100 millions or even billions of elements as the number of elements residing in CPU caches is limited. Therefore, the performance is mainly bound by the overall number of memory transfers required.

Hence, we identify three requirements for main-memory index structures, particularly in the case of large real world datasets. First, the data structure has to be space efficient. Second, it has to consider cache hierarchies of contemporary CPUs. Third, it has to support incremental updates as read-only indexes are only appropriate for a limited number of use cases.

Currently two categories of main-memory indexes, which address some of these issues, can be identified. On the one hand, read-only index structures like FAST [13] provide cache-conscious search operations as well as decent space utilization, but do not support update operations. On the other hand, main-memory index structures like ART [15] or the CSB^+-Tree [20] provide cache-conscious search as well as update operations, but provide only limited capabilities in terms of space utilization. However, to the best of our knowledge no method satisfying all three requirements exists, which provides space efficiency, cache-conscious design and update functionality.

Therefore, we present the Delta Cache Conscious B-Tree (DCB-Tree) combining cache-conscious operations with efficient space utilization. It is a main-memory B-Tree [3] based index structure tailored for the storage of short fixed-size keys. A hierarchical cache-line aligned node layout reduces the number of cache-misses and the delta encoding of keys along this hierarchical layout reduces the amount of space needed for each entry.

Hence, our contributions in this paper are:

– The main-memory Delta Cache Conscious B-Tree (*DCB-Tree*)-Tree. It is a space efficient, cache-conscious index for the storage of short fixed size keys.
– Novel algorithms for lookup and insertion, which are specific for the *DCB-Tree*.
– An evaluation of the *DCB-Tree*, which shows that the *DCB-Tree* provides superior space utilization, while providing equal or better performance for large real world datasets.

The remainder of this paper is structured as follows. Section 2 discusses the related work. Section 3 introduces the *DCB-Tree*, its structure and the algorithms used. Section 4 presents the evaluation and its results. Section 5 draws a conclusion and gives a short overview about future work.

2 Related Work

The work presented in this paper is related to the area of index structures and index compression techniques.

In the area of index structures allowing sequential access, comparison-based tree structures as well as trie-based index structures prevailing. The B-Tree [3,8] represents the dominating disk based index structure and is the basis of many relational database systems. While variations of binary search trees like the Red Black Tree [2,11] or the T-Tree [14] were the dominating main-memory index structures until the 1990's, Rao et al. [19] showed that B-Tree based structures exceed binary tree index structures due to their better cache-line utilization. Rao et al. further presented the CSB+ tree [20], which optimizes cache-line utilization by reducing the number of pointers through offset calculation in the index part. While the CSB+ tree improves memory utilization, no key or pointer compression was applied. Due to the fact that cache optimized trees provide only limited performance when used as disc based structures, Chen et al. presented the Fractal Prefetching B^+-Tree [7], which facilitates a hierarchical cache-optimized layout optimizing disc as well as main memory performance.

Another approach aiming for a cacheline optimization is the BW-Tree [16] by Levandoski et al. which is optimized for high concurrency by facilitating atomic compare and swap operations instead of locks. A further direction of research is to facilitate the data-parallel features of modern hardware to improve the search operation within the tree nodes. The Fast Architecture Sensitive Tree (FAST) by Kim et al. [13] and the k-array search based approach by Schlegel et al. [21] use SIMD operations to speed up search operations. While it was shown that both trees provide improved search performance, they were designed as read-only index lacking update operations. Another approach to speed up the search operation is to use trie-based index structures [9]. However, a major drawback of tries is the worst-case space consumption. The Adaptive Radix Tree (ART) [15] by Leis et al. represents a trie variation dedicated to modern hardware, which mitigates this worst-case space consumption by using adaptive node sizes as well as a hybrid approach for path compression. Moreover, the authors showed that the ART tree is able to outperform FAST and under certain conditions also hashtables. Another approach based on tries is the Masstree [17] by Mao et al., which is a trie with fanout 2^{64} where each trie node is represented by a B^+-Tree storing an 8 byte portion of the key. This design results in good performance for long shared prefixes.

In the domain of index compression techniques several different approaches to compress the index part as well as the file part of B-Trees were developed. The reason is that the performance of index structures is heavily bound by the branching factor. A common compression scheme related to the compression of the index part is prefix or rear compression. The prefix B-Tree [4] by Bayer and Unterauer uses prefix compression on a bit level to only store partial keys in the index part of the tree. Furthermore, they soften the B-Tree properties to select partial keys with the shortest length. Bohannon et al. extended the concept of partial keys in their pkT-trees and pkB-trees [6] to improve cache and search performance. In the index part they use fixed size portions of the prefix to optimistically compare with the search key. If the comparison cannot be performed, a pointer to the full index key is dereferenced. The authors point out that the partial key is superior in terms of performance for larger keys only. While this scheme improves the cache-line utilization, it imposes a memory overhead due to the overhead of the pointer as well as the partial key itself. A more recent approach for using partial keys was incorporated in FAST [13]. It compresses the index keys by applying a SIMD based approach to only store those bits that actually differ.

3   DCB-Tree

In this section, we present the Delta Cache Conscious B-Tree (*DCB-Tree*). The major goal of the DCB-Tree is to store fixed size keys of sizes up to 8 bytes in the *DCB8-Tree* and keys of up to 16 bytes in the larger *DCB16-Tree*. Further aims of the *DCB-Tree* are a low memory footprint, update ability and taking cache hierarchies into account to provide decent performance. The two variations *DCB8-Tree* and the *DCB16-Tree* differ only in the underlying integer type. The reason that two versions exist, is that the 8 byte integer type is mapped to a native data type and therefore provides better performance compared to the custom 16 byte integer type. In the following, we will use the term *DCB-Tree* synonymously for both the *DCB8-Tree* and the *DCB16-Tree*.

The intended use of the *DCB-Tree* is to provide a clustered in-memory index for short fixed-length keys, which occur in triple stores or inverted indexes. Due to the dataset sizes in those areas, the *DCB-Tree* focuses primarily on the reduction of the overall memory footprint to ensure that datasets can be processed in main-memory only. To reduce the memory footprint, the *DCB-Tree* exhibits the circumstance that generally keys are not randomly distributed. Moreover, in real world scenarios coherence can be found in the datasets. This circumstance is utilized by the *DCB-Tree* for the encoding of keys and for the encoding of pointers. The *DCB-Tree* is an n-ary search tree incorporating ideas of B-Trees [3], B^+-Trees [8] and CSB^+-Trees [20]. Values are only stored at the leaf-level. Due to the fact that the *DCB-Tree* is designed as a clustered index structure, no pointers to the actual record are stored on the leaf node level. In the following we describe the node and bucket layout, discuss the pointer encoding and memory layout and explain the algorithms for lookup and insertion.

3.1   Two Stage Node Layout

Each node, index node as well as leaf node, has a two stage layout. The first stage is the header section and the second stage consists of the buckets containing the content (keys). Furthermore, each node has an implicit offset which is defined by its corresponding parent node entry. In the case of the root node, the offset is defined to be zero. An example node layout is illustrated in Fig. 1.

The header section of each node contains header-entries (H_1-H_n), which are uncompressed keys used as separators between buckets. For instance, header-entry H_1 is larger than any key (K_i) in $Bucket_1$ but smaller or equal to the smallest key in $Bucket_2$. In this way the header-entries can be used to determine

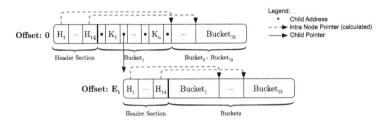

Fig. 1. DCB-tree layout overview

the address of the corresponding bucket address. In Fig. 1 this relationship is visualized by the intra node pointers. However, these intra node pointers are not stored but are calculated relative to the node's base address. Hence, for nodes with header sections containing at most n header-entries at most $n + 1$ buckets are supported. In the case of the DCB-Tree the size of the header section as well as the size of each bucket is determined to two cache-lines. The reason is that the hardware prefetchers[1] of modern CPUs automatically fetch the adjacent cache-line in case of a cache miss. As the number of bytes required per header entry is equal to the maximum key length, headers in a *DCB16*-Tree are twice as large as in a *DCB8-Tree*. Therefore, to be able to address the same number of buckets as in a *DCB8-Tree*'s node the header section of a *DCB16*-Tree spans four cache-lines. As the header-entries are used to address the corresponding buckets, no more than 16 content buckets can be used without increasing the header section size. To ensure that each node is page aligned and that no TLB-miss occurs during the processing of a single node, the node size is fixed to 2kiB. Furthermore the 2kiB node size is tailored to the address translation covered in Sect. 3.3. This node design ensures that at most two cache misses occur on each tree level of a *DCB8-Tree*. In a *DCB16-Tree* this depends on the prefetch policy of the CPU, but tends to three cache misses.

3.2   Bucket Structure

As described in the previous section, the content of each node is stored in its buckets. To distinguish buckets located in index nodes from buckets located in leaf nodes, we denote buckets in index nodes as index buckets and buckets in leaf nodes as leaf buckets. Due to the fact that the bucket structure is similar to the node structure in B^+-Trees we only discuss the properties which are different from the B^+-Tree's node structure.

Index buckets contain keys and pointers to the corresponding subtree. Each index bucket contains a header section and a content section. The header section stores the number of entries in the content section and the encoding information for keys and pointers. The encoding information for pointers consists of the number of bytes (*Pointer Bytes*) used to store the largest pointer in the bucket.

---

[1] http://tinyurl.com/on8ccx3.

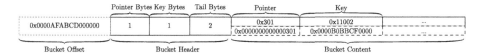

Fig. 2. Index bucket entry

Keys in index buckets are generated in the course of leaf node splits, such that the lower bytes tend to be zero. Therefore a tail compression is applied on the bucket's keys and the minimum number of tail zero bytes (*Tail Bytes*) is stored in the bucket's header section. Furthermore, the keys are delta coded relative to the bucket's offset and placed in its content section. The maximum number of bytes, which is required to store such an encoded keys, is put into the bucket's header section (*Key Bytes*). An example illustrating pointer as well as key encoding for an index bucket can be seen in Fig. 2. In this figure solid boxes represent stored values, while dashed boxes represent calculated values. For instance, the bucket offset is inferred during tree traversal. Dashed boxes below pointers or keys contain their decoded representations.

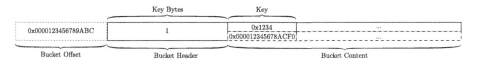

Fig. 3. Leaf bucket entry

Leaf buckets store keys only. Hence their section contains the number of keys in the content section and the information used to encode them. As keys contained within a leaf bucket are highly coherent, the same fixed-length delta based encoding as used for index buckets can be applied. Therefore, the encoding information consists of the maximum number of bytes needed to encode a single key. This is equal to the number of bytes required to encode the leaf bucket's largest key. An example which illustrates the encoding of a leaf bucket can be seen in Fig. 3. The semantics of the dashed and solid boxes is analogous to Fig. 2.

3.3 Pointer Encoding and Memory Layout

It has previously been shown [19] that a large portion of space within index nodes is dedicated to pointer information. Since 64-bit architectures have become mainstream, the space dedicated to pointers has an even higher impact. Therefore, we try to reduce the amount of space dedicated to pointer information with a twofold strategy. On the one hand, the number of pointers required is reduced. This is done by designing the data structure as a clustered index for short fixed sized keys, which eliminates the need for pointers at the leaf node level. Furthermore, by facilitating the nested node layout described in Sect. 3.1, intra-node pointers are eliminated. This approach is similar to the concept of node groups in CSB^+-Trees. On the other hand, the space occupied by each pointer is reduced. This is achieved by using node IDs instead of absolute pointers. Even in the case of huge datasets spanning hundreds of billion of entries, 4 bytes for addressing a single node is sufficient. Therefore, a custom memory allocator is used, which allocates fixed node size chunks from a pool of large buffers and is able to translate node IDs to absolute addresses. The overhead of calculating the absolute node address is negligible, as 2^n sized buffers are used.

3.4   Algorithms

As a *DCB-Trees* resembles a special version of a B-Tree, the basic algorithms for insertion and update are the same. The huge difference in comparison to standard B-Trees is that each node features a two stage layout, with key and pointer compression on a per bucket basis. We therefore describe only the parts of the algorithms and operations that are different compared to B-Trees and B^+-Trees [3,8]. Moreover, only insertion as well as lookup operations are considered. Nonetheless, algorithms for delete operations can be inferred analogously.

Lookup. In the case of a lookup operation, the two stage node layout results in the following three steps, which are needed for searching a node.

1. A linear search is executed on the node's header to determine the corresponding bucket and its offset. The bucket offset of the first bucket is equal to the node offset. In any other case, the bucket offset is equal to the largest header entry which is smaller or equal to the search key.
2. The search key is encoded. Therefore, the bucket offset is subtracted from the search key. In the case of an index bucket, the search key is tail encoded to match the encoding of the bucket to search.
3. A lookup operation is executed on the bucket using the encoded search key. In the case of an index bucket search, the key preceding the matching pointer becomes the node offset in the next search step.

Insert. To insert a key into a *DCB-Tree*, first the target leaf bucket is determined by the lookup operation explained in the previous paragraph. Second, it is determined whether sufficient space is available to insert the key and whether a potential recode operation succeeds. Such a recode operation is required if the new key is larger than any existing entry in the bucket. If both conditions can be satisfied, the bucket is encoded and the key inserted. If one of the conditions fail, the following overflow handling strategies are applied in the given order.

1. In the case of inserting keys in ascending order, buckets tend to be only half full. To prevent this situation, keys are rotated to the left sibling bucket, if sufficient space is available. This corresponds to a local rotation.
2. Otherwise a bucket split becomes necessary. Unless the node is full, the bucket split is executed and the minimum key of the right bucket is inserted as a new separator in the node's header section.
3. If a bucket split cannot be performed and the left sibling node can contain further buckets, buckets are locally rotated to the left sibling node and the

insertion is retried. In the case of a bucket rotation the node offset must be recalculated, which can lead to another bucket split. Furthermore, the new node offset must be propagated to the parent node.

4. If no bucket rotation can be applied a node split is required. The buckets are distributed, the node offset for the right node is calculated and the pointer to the right node together with its offset is inserted into the parent node.

For the generation of the node offset, in case of a leaf-node split, Algorithm 1 is used. It calculates a separator between the left and the right node with as many trailing zero bytes as possible. Moreover, it does not calculate the shortest common prefix between the largest left and the lowest right value, as in case of the prefix B-Tree [4], but the shortest common prefix between the mean value of both values and the lowest right value. The reason is that it tries to balance the size of the right node's first bucket values while still providing a decent prefix.

Algorithm 1. Tail Compressible Mean

1: **procedure** TAILCOMPRESSIBLEMEAN($lower, upper$)
2:     $mean \leftarrow (upper + lower)/2$
3:     $upperMask \leftarrow -1l \ggg numberOfLeadingZeros(upper)$
4:     $tailCompressableBits = log_2((mean \oplus upper) \wedge upperMask)$
5:     **return** $(-1l \ll tailCompressableBits) \wedge upper$
6: **end procedure**

---

4   Evaluation

In this section we evaluate the *DCB-Tree*. Therefore we conduct two benchmarks. The first compares the memory consumptions with other main-memory data structures. The second evaluates the runtime performance.

4.1   Benchmark Environment

All benchmarks are executed on the Java Runtime Environment version 1.8.0_05 with the following system properties set: `-XX:NewRatio=3 -Xmx90g -Xms40g -XX:+UseConcMarkSweepGC -XX:MaxDirectMemorySize=90g`.

For the evaluation we used a server with an Intel Xeon L5520 running at a clock speed of 2.27 GHz clock speed, 64 KB L1 cache per core, 256 KB L2 cache per core and 8MB L3 shared cache. The server has 96 GB of DDR3/1066 RAM and runs CentOS 6.5 with Linux Kernel 2.6.32.

4.2   Evaluated Data Structures

As the *DCB-Tree* is implemented in Java, all benchmarks are evaluated on the Java Platform. The implementation of the DCB-Tree is available online[2]. We

---

[2] http://dbis-informatik.uibk.ac.at/static/ma/robert/imdm/imdm2014.zip.

evaluated the two variations *DCB8-Tree* and *DCB16-Tree*. Due to the lack of built-in 16 byte wide integers a custom integer data type is used as the underlying data type for the *DCB16-Tree*.

As contestants, the TreeSet[3] representing the Java Platform's standard implementation of a Red-Black Tree [11] and a port of the ART Tree [15] were used. As the ART tree is originally available as C++ implementation[4] we created a port for the Java Language, which is available online. Due to the lack of SIMD operations on the Java Platform, the lookup in the nodes containing up to 16 keys of the ART Tree had to be implemented by linear search. Although it is expected that the ART port is slower than the C++ implementation due to the overhead incurred by the Java Virtual Machine, the same overhead is applied to all contestants. For keys up to the length of 8 bytes the key is encoded inside the pointer as it is the case in the original implementation. The reason is that 8 bytes are already reserved for the pointer. In the case of keys larger than 8 bytes the ART Tree is used as a secondary index structure as the 16 byte key cannot be encoded in an 8 byte pointer.

It is important to note, that in the case of the ART Tree as well as the DCB-Tree, pointers represent relative offsets in a direct ByteBuffer[5]. This is similar to an offset for an array in C.

4.3   Datasets

In the scenario of keys up to 8 bytes length we use three different datasets. The first dataset contains dense values ranging from 0 to n. The second dataset contains random values. Finally, two real world dataset are used. On the one hand side triples of the Yago2 dataset [12] are encoded as 8 byte sized keys in the following way: The lowest 26 bits are used for the object id. Bits 27 to 37 store the predicate information and the bits ranging from 38 to 63 are used for the subject information. On the other hand triples from the DBpedia [1] dataset version 3.9 are encoded as 16 byte sized key. Each triple is encoded in a single 16 byte integer, such that the lowest 4 bytes represent the object id, the next 4 bytes the predicate id and the next 4 bytes the subject id.

For the sake of simplicity we subsequently denote these four datasets as *Dense*, *Random*, *Yago* and *DBpedia*.

4.4   Memory Consumption

To evaluate the memory consumption we insert 10 K, 100 K, 1 M, 10 M and 100 M keys of each dataset into the index structures and measure the space consumption for each structure. For *DBpedia*, we use dataset sizes ranging from 100 K up to 1 B keys. The space consumption is summarized in Table 1, with the best values written in bold. This table presents the bytes used per entry

---

[3] http://docs.oracle.com/javase/8/docs/api/java/util/TreeSet.html.

[4] http://www-db.in.tum.de/~leis/index/ART.tgz?lang=de.

[5] http://docs.oracle.com/javase/8/docs/api/java/nio/ByteBuffer.html.

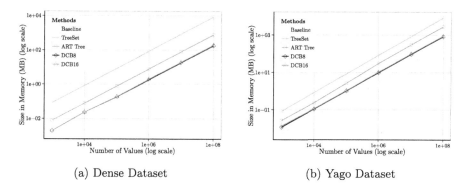

(a) Dense Dataset   (b) Yago Dataset

Fig. 4. Memory consumption

for 100 million randomly inserted keys of each data set. Moreover the *Baseline* value used in Table 1 represents the bytes needed per key, given all keys are delta coded relative to their direct predecessor and encoded with a byte-level fixed-prefix encoding. Furthermore the memory consumption is exemplarily visualized for *Dense* in Fig. 4a and for *Yago* in Fig. 4b.

As it can be seen in both Figures, as well as in Table 1, the overhead in terms of memory consumption between *DCB8* and *DCB16* is negligible and can be explained by the additional cache-lines used in the header section of *DCB16*. Hence, in the rest of this subsection we will use *DCB* synonymously for *DCB8* and *DCB16*.

The results of all experiments show that the *DCB*-Tree has the best space utilization of the evaluated data structures. In the best case (*Dense*) it uses 30 % more space than the Baseline. Even in the worst case it uses only three times more space compared to the Baseline. The DCB-Tree uses between two third of the memory of the second best index structure (ART-Tree) in the case of *Random*, and up to five times less space in the case of *DBpedia*. In the case of *DBpedia* it has to be considered that the keys cannot be stored inside ART. Therefore 16 bytes of the 60 bytes per entry are dedicated to the storage of the keys itself. Considering only the space required for the index part, the *DCB*-Tree uses only one third of the space. It can be seen in Table 1 that this ratio is equal for *Yago*, which represents a scale-free network as well. In all experiments it can be seen that the TreeSet performs worst. For each dataset it consumes about an

Table 1. Memory consumption per key for TreeSet, ArtTree and DCB in datasets of 100 million values

Dataset	Baseline	TreeSet	δ_{Tree}	ArtTree	δ_{Art}	DCB8	δ_{DCB8}	DCB16	δ_{DCB16}
Dense	1.5	88	58.67	8.1	5.4	1.89	**1.26**	2.03	1.35
Yago	3.2	88	27.5	29.4	9.19	8.73	**2.73**	9.36	2.92
Randomt	5.45	88	16.15	18.67	3.43	11.23	**2.06**	12.04	2.21
DBPedia	3.78	96	25.4	60.01	15.88	NA	NA	12.66	**3.35**

order of magnitude more space per key than the *DCB*-Tree. The reason is that it uses no compression and has a poor payload-to-pointer ratio.

4.5   Runtime Performance

To evaluate the runtime behavior, the same datasets and sizes as in the memory benchmark are used. For each configuration, 100,000,000 lookup operations are issued in a random order and the number of operations performed per second are measured. The results for *Dense* is shown in Fig. 5a, for *Random* in Fig. 5c, for *Yago* in Fig. 5b and for *DBpedia* in Fig. 5d. It can be observed that regarding the artificial datasets *Dense* and *Random*, the ART Tree processes about 50 % more lookups per second than the *DCB8* tree. Although the Red Black Tree has very good performance for datasets having less than 10,000 entries, for larger datasets the performance drops significantly and is surpassed by both the *DCB*-Tree as well as the ART-Tree.

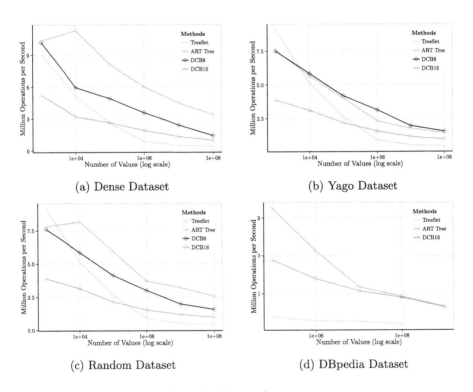

(a) Dense Dataset   (b) Yago Dataset

(c) Random Dataset   (d) DBpedia Dataset

Fig. 5. Lookup performance

In case of the large real world datasets *Yago* and *DBpedia* the DCB-Tree is on the same level or superior to the ART Tree. For *Yago*, depending on the dataset size, DCB8 processes between 7 % and 30 % more operations per second than ART. For *DBpedia*, *DCB-16* has an equivalent runtime performance as ART for more than 10,000,000 entries. The reason that *DCB-16* performs up to 50 % worse than ART for dataset sizes smaller than 10,000,000, is the overhead of the custom 16 byte integer implementation, as no native 16 byte integer datatype is available on the Java Platform. ART is not affected by this, because it performs a byte wise comparison. Nevertheless, due to its tree height and the increased number of cache misses, the performance of ART drops significantly for datasets larger than 10,000,000 entries.

The reason that the TreeSet is only evaluated for dataset sizes of up to 100,000,000 entries is that the amount of memory required exceeds the amount of RAM available in our benchmark environment (more than 96 GB).

5   Conclusion and Future Work

In this paper we presented the DCB-Tree, a cache-conscious index structure for the storage of short fixed size keys. The DCB-Tree combines a hierarchical cache aligned node layout with delta encoding and pointer compression. The evaluation results show the best memory utilization among the contestants, while providing equal or better performance for large real world datasets.

We presented algorithms for insertion and search operations and described the influence of the two-stage node layout on B-Tree operations. Furthermore, the DCB-Tree was evaluated against two other index structures, namely the ART Tree and a Red Black Tree on artificial as well as on real world datasets. We show that for dense as well as for large real world dataset the DCB-Tree requires only 20 % of memory compared to other state of the art index structures. Moreover, our evaluation shows that the DCB-Tree provides decent performance using artificial datasets. In the case of large real world datasets it is equivalent or superior to state of the art in-memory index structure ART, while providing a more efficient space consumption. In future work, we will investigate other encoding strategies to further reduce the amount of memory required. Furthermore, we plan to integrate the DCB-Tree into RDF-Stores as well as to use it as a basis for full text indexes.

References

1. Auer, S., Bizer, C., Kobilarov, G., Lehmann, J., Cyganiak, R., Ives, Z.: DBpedia: a nucleus for a web of open data. In: Aberer, K., et al. (eds.) ISWC/ASWC 2007. LNCS, vol. 4825, pp. 722–735. Springer, Heidelberg (2007)
2. Bayer, R.: Symmetric binary B-Trees: data structure and maintenance algorithms. Acta Informatica **1**(4), 290–306 (1972)
3. Bayer, R., McCreight, E.: Organization and maintenance of large ordered indices. In: Proceedings of the SIGFIDET (now SIGMOD) 1970, p. 107. ACM Press, New York (1970)
4. Bayer, R., Unterauer, K.: Prefix B-Trees. ACM Trans. Database Syst. **2**(1), 11–26 (1977)

5. Binna, R., Gassler, W., Zangerle, E., Pacher, D., Specht, G.: SpiderStore: exploiting main memory for efficient RDF graph representation and fast querying. In: Proceedings of Workshop on Semantic Data Management (SemData) at VLDB (2010)

6. Bohannon, P., McIlroy, P., Rastogi, R.: Main-memory index structures with fixed-size partial keys. In: Proceedings of SIGMOD 2001, vol. 30, pp. 163–174. ACM Press, New York, June 2001

7. Chen, S., Gibbons, P.B., Mowry, T.C., Valentin, G.: Fractal prefetching B+-Trees. In: Proceedings of SIGMOD 2002, p. 157. ACM Press, New York (2002)

8. Comer, D.: Ubiquitous B-Tree. ACM Comput. Surv. **11**(2), 121–137 (1979)

9. Fredkin, E.: Trie memory. Commun. ACM **3**(9), 490–499 (1960)

10. Gray, J.: Tape is dead, disk is tape, flash is disk, RAM locality is king, Gong Show Presentation at CIDR (2007)

11. Guibas, L.J., Sedgewick, R.: A dichromatic framework for balanced trees. In: 19th Annual Symposium on Foundations of Computer Science (SCFS 1978), pp. 8–21. IEEE, October 1978

12. Hoffart, J., Suchanek, F.M., Berberich, K., Lewis-Kelham, E., de Melo, G., Weikum, G.: YAGO2: exploring and querying world knowledge in time, space, context, and many languages. In: Proceedings of WWW 2011, p. 229. ACM Press, New York (2011)

13. Kim, C., Chhugani, J., Satish, N., Sedlar, E., Nguyen, A.D., Kaldewey, T., Lee, V.W., Brandt, S.A., Dubey, P.: FAST: fast architecture sensitive tree search on Modern CPUs and GPUs. In: Proceedings of SIGMOD 2010, p. 339 (2010)

14. Lehman, T.J., Careay, M.J.: A study of index structures for main memory database management systems. In: Proceedings of VLDB 1986, pp. 294–303 (1986)

15. Leis, V., Kemper, A., Neumann, T.: The adaptive radix tree: ARTful indexing for main-memory databases. In: Proceedings of ICDE 2013, pp. 38–49. IEEE, April 2013

16. Levandoski, J.J., Lomet, D.B., Sengupta, S.: The Bw-tree: A B-tree for new hardware platforms. In: Proceedings of ICDE 2013, pp. 302–313 (2013)

17. Mao, Y., Kohler, E., Morris, R.T.: Cache craftiness for fast multicore key-value storage. In: Proceedings of the 7th ACM European Conference on Computer Systems - EuroSys 2012, p. 183 (2012)

18. Neumann, T., Weikum, G.: RDF-3X: a RISC-style engine for RDF. In: Proceedings of VLDB Endowment, vol. 1, pp. 647–659, August 2008

19. Rao, J., Ross, K.A.: Cache Conscious Indexing for Decision-Support in Main Memory. In: Proceedings of VLDB 1999, pp. 475–486. Morgan Kaufmann Publishers Inc. (1999)

20. Rao, J., Ross, K.A.: Making B+-Trees cache conscious in main memory. ACM SIGMOD Rec. **29**(2), 475–486 (2000)

21. Schlegel, B., Gemulla, R., Lehner, W.: k-ary search on modern processors. In: Proceedings of the Fifth International Workshop on Data Management on New Hardware - DaMoN 2009, p. 52. ACM Press, New York (2009)

22. Wulf, W.A., McKee, S.A.: Hitting the memory wall. ACM SIGARCH Comput. Archit. News **23**(1), 20–24 (1995)

Composite Group-Keys

Space-Efficient Indexing of Multiple Columns for Compressed In-Memory Column Stores

Martin Faust$^{(\boxtimes)}$, David Schwalb, and Hasso Plattner

Hasso Plattner Institute for IT Systems Engineering,
University of Potsdam, Potsdam, Germany
{martin.faust,david.schwalb,hasso.plattner}@hpi.de

Abstract. Real world applications make heavy use of composite keys to reference entities. Indices over multiple columns are therefore mandatory to achieve response time goals of applications. We describe and evaluate the Composite Group-Key Index for fast tuple retrieval via composite keys from the compressed partition of in-memory column-stores with a main/delta architecture. Composite Group-Keys work directly on the dictionary-encoded columns. Multiple values are encoded in a native integer and extended by an inverted index. The proposed index offers similar lookup performance as alternative approaches, but reduces the storage requirements significantly. For our analyzed dataset of an enterprise application the index can reduce the storage footprint compared to B+Trees by 70 percent. We give a detailed study of the lookup performance for a variable number of attributes and show that the index can be created efficiently by working directly on the dictionary-compressed data.

1 Introduction

Today's hardware is available in configurations and at price points that make in-memory database systems a viable choice for many applications in enterprise computing. We focus on columnar in-memory storage with a write-optimized delta partition and a larger read-optimized main partition. This architecture supports high performance analytical queries [2,12], while still allowing for sufficient transactional performance [5]. The results from an analysis of all primary keys of a large enterprise resource planning (ERP) system installation provide the input for the evaluation of different indexing techniques. The Composite Group-Key index is built on top of multiple dictionary-encoded columns by storing compact key-identifiers derived from the encoded representation of the key's fields. The key-identifiers maintain the sort order of the tuples and therefore, the index supports range lookups, which have a significant share in enterprise workloads [5].

Applications use composite keys to model entities according to their real world counterpart and the relationships between them. Redesigning database schemata to avoid the usage of composite keys is cumbersome and often contrary

© Springer International Publishing Switzerland 2015
A. Jagatheesan et al. (Eds.): IMDM 2013/2014, LNCS 8921, pp. 139–150, 2015.
DOI: 10.1007/978-3-319-13960-9_11

to the goal of achieving a good abstraction of entities. To avoid the high costs of composite keys, database designs might use surrogate keys. However, the introduction of surrogate keys brings new problems, such as a disassociation of the key and the actual data and problems of uniquely referencing entities, among others. This is also visible in industry benchmarks like the TPC-C: of the nine tables in the TPC-C schema, seven have a composite key, two thereof have additional, secondary composite indices. TPC-H's largest table *lineitems* has a composite key as well. Consequently, nearly all row-based relational database systems support composite indices. Looking at the internal record based storage scheme of row stores, the support for composite indices is a straightforward extension of the single attribute index. The primary key is often automatically set as the cluster key of the table, e.g. it establishes the sort order of a table on disk.

In-memory column stores with a main/delta architecture like Hyrise [4] and SAP HANA [12] keep the majority of the data in highly compressed, read-only partitions. Therefore, an additional index on record-level on such partitions can impose a significant part of the overall storage consumption of a table. To maintain a high query performance, the main and delta partition is combined into a new compressed main partition whenever the delta partition grows too large. To keep this merge process simple and fast and the compression scheme flexible, we do not consider the tables to be kept in the sort order of the primary key [5]. Consequently, a separate index structure is needed to enforce uniqueness constraints and fast single tuple access.

In the following sections, we describe the Composite Group-Key Index and benchmark it against alternative indexing schemes for the dictionary-compressed main partition of in-memory column stores with regard to their storage consumption and applicability in a real world enterprise application. We show that the lookup performance of Composite Group-Keys can keep up with alternative implementations while imposing a significantly smaller space overhead. A detailed analysis of a large enterprise application with several thousand tables and billions of records shows its applicability and limitations.

2   Real World Enterprise Application: SAP ERP

An Enterprise Resource Planning (ERP) application is the central planning software for large companies. It typically stores all invoices, sales orders, deliveries, and general ledger documents, and the connections between them, among other relevant data. We had the opportunity to obtain a complete system copy from a large, productive installation of the SAP ERP application from a Fortune 500 company. Although the analysis of a single instance of the product does not cover the entire ERP market, we believe that the findings are valuable and applicable to a larger scope of enterprise applications. The SAP ERP software has about 25 percent market share in the global ERP market and is used by more than half of the Fortune 500 companies. We verified the results from selected tables in a second instance of the application that is used in a different industry.

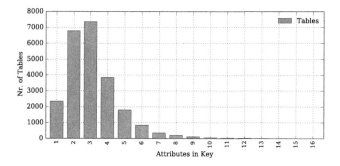

Fig. 1. Analysis of the data in a ERP system from a Fortune 500 company.

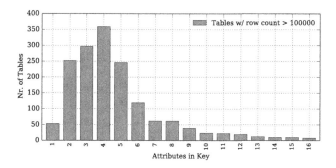

Fig. 2. Number of attributes in primary keys of large tables.

The analyzed ERP system's size is about 5 TB in uncompressed format, it stores 10 billion records in 23886 tables. Each table has a primary key, which is usually a composite key. As an example, the general ledger accounting header's key is composed of the tenant-id, a company code, the document number and the fiscal year. Figure 1 shows number of tables in our database system grouped by the number of attributes in their key, in Fig. 2 a detailed view of the tables with more than 100,000 records is presented. Only 2350 of the 23886 non-empty tables have a primary key of only one attribute, 6789 with two attributes and 14747 have composite keys of three or more attributes. If only the tables with more than 100,000 records are taken into account, 96 percent have a composite key, 81 percent with three or more fields.

Since the application is designed as a multi-tenant system with the tenant-id as the first key in all transactional tables, two keys are the norm. However, even if multi tenancy is implemented on a different layer, there are many more composite keys of higher order. The important finding of the analysis is, that more than 90 percent of the tables have a composite primary key.

Table 1. Symbols

	Symbol		Symbol
Table Length	n	Position List	P
Key-Identifier List	K	Concatenated Key	c
Attribute Vector of Column x	AV_x	Dictionary of Column x	D_x
Column x	C_x	Key-identifier	k_{id}

3   Composite Group-Key

The Composite Group-Key is our proposal for indexing the main partition of in-memory column stores with dictionary compression. Table 1 summarizes the used symbols.

The dictionary compression on the main partition uses sorted dictionaries (D) and bit-packed attribute vectors (AV). We refer to the compressed representation of a value, its bit-packed index into the dictionary, as value-id. Because all dictionaries of the main partition are sorted, the value-ids follow the same sort order as the original values and the value-ids of one column can be directly compared to evaluate the order between values. Therefore, range queries can also be evaluated directly on the compressed format.

The composite Group-Key contains two data structures: a key-identifier list K and a position list P. The key-identifier list contains integer keys k_{id} which are composed of the concatenated value-ids of the respective composite key's values. The bit-wise representation of k_{id} equals the concatenation of the value-ids of the keys fields, as illustrated in Fig. 3(b). The creation of key-identifiers can be implemented efficiently through bit shifts.

The key-identifiers are similar to BLINK's data banks, but as they are composed of fixed-length values, they are binary-comparable across the complete main partition [9]. In the successor, DB2 BLU [8] indices are only used to enforce uniqueness constraints. Best practice guides advice to disable constraint checking, as the B+Tree organized indices consume space and introduce processing overhead[1].

Storage Requirements. The Composite Group-Key maintains two data structures, the key-identifier list K with either 8, 16, 32 or 64 bits per indexed key and a bit-packed position list P. K is always composed of native integer datatypes, to avoid costly bit un-packing during the binary search. P is only accessed to retrieve the respective row-id, hence it is stored with $\lceil \log_2 n \rceil$ bits to save memory space.

---

[1] Rockwood et al.: *Best practices: Optimizing analytic workloads using DB2 10.5 with BLU Acceleration May 2014* on IBM.com.

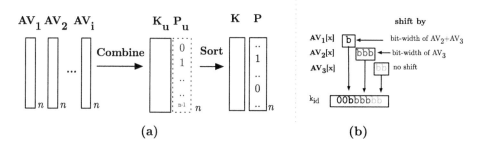

Fig. 3. Composite Group-Key creation: (a) schematic overview, (b) k_{id} creation.

$$K_x = n * \frac{x}{8} \; bytes \mid x \; in \; \{8, 16, 32, 64\} \tag{1}$$

$$P = \frac{\lceil log_2(n) \rceil * n}{8} \; bytes \tag{2}$$

$$Memory_{Comp.GK} = K_x * n + P \tag{3}$$

Key Lookups. The first step of the lookup with the Composite Group-Key Index consists of the translation of all key attributes of the predicate to their respective value-id, using binary search on each key attribute's dictionary. The complexity of each dictionary lookup is $\mathcal{O}((\log |Dict|) * k_i)$, with k_i being the length of the respective key attribute. Afterwards the key-identifier is created by concatenating the value-ids through bit shifts. The search key is used for a binary search on the key-identifier list, which is within $\mathcal{O}(\log n)$. The results, the matching row-id, can be read directly from the offset in P.

Index Creation. The process of creating the index is shown schematically in Fig. 3 and by example in Fig. 4.

In the first step, value-ids from all columns of the composite key are combined to a vector of key-identifiers (K_u). This intermediate data structure is extended by an ascending list of row-ids (P_u). Afterwards both structures are sorted according to the key-identifiers to obtain K and P.

The appropriate native integer type for the key-identifier list is calculated by adding up the length of the value-ids of all indexed attributes and rounding up to the next power of two.

4 Alternative Index Implementations

This section briefly introduces two alternatives for secondary indexing of multiple columns. Both allow the efficient execution of single key and range queries. However, they index the full composite key, instead of a shorter integer representation. Our goal is to show, that it is viable to transform the key into its compressed representation, although a binary search on each dictionary is necessary before searching for the actual key-identifier.

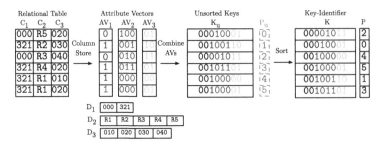

Fig. 4. Composite Group-Key creation: Example with 8 bit integer key-identifier.

4.1   Tuple-Based B+tree

A classic implementation of an index stores pairs of the actual composite key and a row-id in a tree structure. Since the tree stores the uncompressed keys, no additional dictionary lookups have to be performed upfront, and the search takes place directly on the tree. The drawback of this approach is the need for expensive comparisons of the actual composite key while traversing the tree and its higher storage requirements (roughly 2x the data [11]) for internal pointers. Newer trie-based structures, such as the Generalized Prefix Trees proposed by Böhm et al. [1] and further developed in the Adaptive Radix Tree (ART) by Leis et al. [6] address some of the problems that classic B+Trees have. However, also tries require the replication of keys in the index and additional space for auxiliary structures.

For a basic performance comparison, we use the STX B+Tree library[2], a drop in STL map replacement, which is optimized for modern CPUs and more storage efficient than the GNU STL red-black trees. C++ tuples of char-arrays are used to store the key. The number of attributes in the key is a template parameter, i.e. there is no additional runtime overhead to determine the number of keys.

Storage Requirements. For our comparison we ignore the internal overhead of the B+Tree's structures, and only assume that the indexed keys are replicated once into the tree structure, and an additional 8 bytes for the row-id pointer are stored. The resulting value is a lower-bound for any indexing scheme that replicates the keys into the index structure without further compression of the keys or row-id pointers.

$$Memory_{B+Tree} = (c + 8) * n \text{ bytes} \qquad (4)$$

Key Lookups. To find the corresponding row-ids for a predicate on the composite key, the key's attributes are concatenated to a single search key. In our implementation a fixed-length byte-array is indexed. To search the index for

---

[2] http://panthema.net/2007/stx-btree/.

matches, the byte-array has to be created from the query predicates. Then, a search on the tree is performed and the row-id is read from the leaf. Let k be the length of the composite key, e.g. the sum of the length of all attributes that form the key. The complexity of building the key is within $\mathcal{O}(k)$ and the actual search on the index within $\mathcal{O}(log(n) * k)$, since the key comparison is in itself a $\mathcal{O}(k)$ operation.

4.2   Concatenated Attribute with Inverted Index

An alternative implementation to index composite primary keys adds an additional column to the table. The additional column holds concatenated values of all key attributes. It is extended by an inverted index to allow for fast tuple retrieval through the concatenated key. This essentially creates a clustered in-memory row store for the vertical partition of the composite key, and allows other database operations, like joins and aggregations, to work on the single concatenated column instead of handling multiple columns. Its integration into existing analytical column store engines without indices promises to be feasible with less effort than the introduction of new data structures and operators. If the key is composed of fixed length fields, the concatenated values follow the same sort order as the original values, otherwise a specialized encoding scheme has to be employed to support range queries. If a primary key is indexed, the resulting column has 100 percent distinct values and the dictionary is essentially an uncompressed representation of the Composite Group-Keys key-identifier list.

Storage Requirements. The concatenated key column consists of a sorted dictionary of string-keys (D), the attribute vector (AV) and a bit-packed position list (P). For primary keys the resulting key column has 100 percent distinct values, therefore we avoid adding a level of indirection [3] to cope with differently sized position lists, and instead store the positions directly in P. The differences to the B+Tree lower-bound stem from the bit-packed row-ids, an optimization that is only possible, if row-ids are stored consecutively. The resulting size is dominated by the dictionary, which is further compressed in practice. Müller et al. [7] inspect the compression of the dictionary, and report compression factors between two and eight [7]. We show the results of the uncompressed column, as well as with a dictionary compression factor four.

$$AV_{Concat} = \frac{\lceil log_2(n) \rceil * n}{8bit} \ bytes \tag{5}$$

$$D_{Concat} = n * sizeof(c) \tag{6}$$

$$P = \frac{\lceil log_2(n) \rceil * n}{8} \ bytes \tag{7}$$

$$Memory_{Concat} = AV_{Concat} + D_{Concat} + P \tag{8}$$

$$Memory_{CompressedConcat} = AV_{Concat} + 0.25 * D_{Concat} + P \tag{9}$$

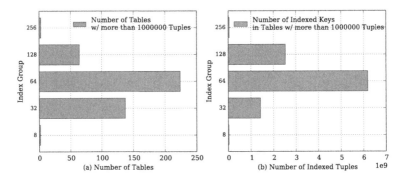

Fig. 5. Large tables from the ERP system by their respective Composite Group-Key class.

Key Lookups. A predicate on the key columns is translated to the concatenated version of the composite key by the query processor, similar to query processing with B+Trees. Next, a binary search for the concatenated key is performed on the concatenated column's dictionary. The respective row-id is obtained from the inverted index through a direct offset lookup in constant time. The lookup complexity is equal to the B+Tree lookup.

5   Evaluation

We compare the different indices with regard to the storage requirements, lookup performance, and index rebuild costs.

5.1   Storage Requirements of ERP Primary Keys

We use the insights from the ERP dataset analysis to compare the expected storage footprints of the Composite Group-Key Index and the presented alternatives.

To evaluate the applicability of our proposed Composite Group-Key index we calculate the size of the key-identifier for all tables: Fig. 5(a) shows the aggregated counts of the tables that are found in the system and have more than one million rows, and Fig. 5(b) the indexed tuples within these tables. It highlights the importance of the 32 bit and 64 bit index cases, however, 86 tables of the analyzed dataset would need a 128 or 256 bit key-identifier, if the Composite Group-Key is applied. We focus on the configurations in which an native integer type is sufficient and leave the other cases for future work. Nevertheless, tables that use the Composite Group-Key can still grow at runtime, without leading to problems: as the size of the key-identifier is known at merge-time, the decision to use the Composite Group-Key can be safely made for each table. The limitations cannot be hit during normal query processing, i.e. during insertions or updates, but only when a re-encode of the main partition occurs during the merge process.

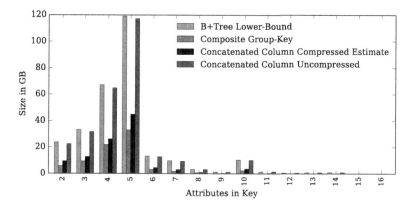

Fig. 6. Calculated index sizes grouped by attributes in key for the 23800 tables of the analyzed ERP system where the Composite Group-Key is applicable.

The total memory footprint of all primary keys in the ERP dataset is 287 GB for the calculated B+Tree lower-bound, 278 GB for the concatenated attribute, 108 GB for the estimate of compressed concatenated column, and 79 GB for the Composite Group-Key Index. The Composite Group-Key has a memory footprint advantage of about 70 percent less than the lower-bound of B+Trees and the uncompressed concatenated attribute. Even with an assumed compression factor of 4 for the dictionary of the concatenated attribute, the Composite Group-Key still leads to a 30 percent reduction. The storage footprint of the concatenated column and the Composite Group-Key are equal at an assumed compression factor of eight for all concatenated dictionaries.

In Fig. 6, we compare the resulting index sizes of the Composite Group-Key Index and the other indexing schemes grouped by the number of fields in the composite key. It shows the storage savings of the Composite Group-Key compared to the presented alternatives. It highlights that most savings in the ERP system can be made in keys with 4 and 5 attributes.

5.2   Lookup Performance

We benchmark the performance of key selects via the index. For each of the introduced indices we randomly pick 100 keys and report the average access time in CPU cycles. The benchmarks include the complete predicate-to-result translation, e.g. in case of the concatenated attribute the predicates are copied to create the char-array search key. For the Group-Key Index a binary search on each dictionary is performed. All measurements were performed on an Intel Core i5-3470 3.2 GHz CPU with 8 GB RAM running Ubuntu 13.10 and using the GCC 4.8.1 compiler. The results are plotted for three to five attributes in the key in Figs. 7 and 8. In Fig. 7, the lookup performance of a single, uncached access to the index is reported. The three index types show a similar performance, with a minimal penalty for the B+Tree. Figure 8 reports the results for 100

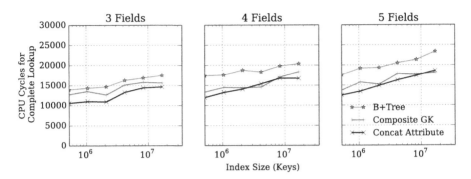

Fig. 7. Uncached Performance of Lookups. The CPU cache has been cleared between each access.

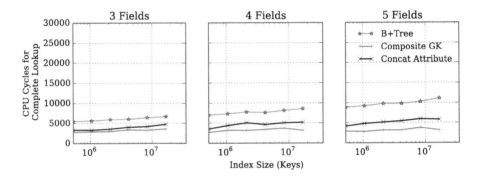

Fig. 8. Cached Performance of Lookups. Same experiment as in Fig. 7 but without invalidation of the CPU cache between runs.

consecutive index accesses to different values without any forced CPU cache invalidation. Here, the smaller size of the Composite Group-Key is beneficial for cache locality, and it outperforms the alternatives consistently. We conclude that the Composite Group-Key's performance is on-par with other established indexing schemes.

5.3   Index Creation and Maintenance

To keep the delta partition small and fast, its contents are merged from time to time into the main partition [5]. Only at *merge time*, the main partition index has to be maintained, as all other write operations during runtime are handled by the delta partition and a special invalidation vector of the main partition.

During the merge process, the delta and main partition are combined to a new main partition, thereby potentially changing the value-ids of every value in the former main store [5]. Additionally, the merge process handles a column at a time, making in difficult to handle composite keys, as multiple columns have to be considered. The merge process runs concurrently to transactions, hence, the

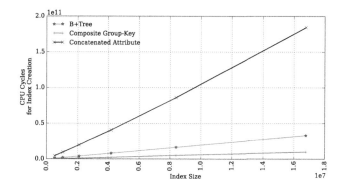

Fig. 9. Index creation performance for different main partition sizes

current index cannot be modified in-place. Therefore, after the merge process created a new main partition, a new index is built from scratch.

This works for all index types, but as Fig. 9 shows, the costs vary. The high costs for the concatenated attribute are due to the expensive byte-wise operations on all values, especially the sorting to create the inverted index. The B+Tree shows better performance due to the better cache locality during the sort. The Composite Group-Key outperforms the two alternative, since it does not work on byte-arrays, but native integers. Since K is a vector of integers, the sorting operation is much faster than the respective sorting of char-arrays.

6   Conclusion and Future Work

We showed the importance of composite keys and proposed a novel index structure tailored towards dictionary encoded column-stores with a main/delta architecture. The Composite Group-Key's lookup performance is on par with other established indexing schemes while significantly reducing the storage footprint for a variety of real world tables. Its implementation leverages the encoding of the primary data by encoding value-ids instead of values. It can therefore avoid costly byte-wise comparisons and perform the comparison of multiple parts of the key in a single integer comparison. Although the Composite Group-Key's lookup complexity suggests that a lookup operation is more costly than in the other cases, its actual performance on modern CPUs keeps up with the alternatives. It is a viable choice to use the compressed representation of a key to perform fast single-tuple lookups in in-memory column-stores with a main/delta architecture.

In future work we plan to evaluate how additional optimizations, such as storing the key-identifier list as a CSS tree [10] or trie compare in this setting. Bit-packing row-ids in tree leaf nodes is another option to reduce the memory footprint of tree structures. Additionally, clustered indices can be applied to our columnar in-memory storage engine. The binary search on the sorted compressed columns is similar to the Composite Group-Key lookup, since the predicate needs to be translated to the compressed representation as well, before the search on the partition can be performed. Nevertheless, additional index structures could improve search performance on the sorted table.

References

1. Böhm, M., Schlegel, B., Volk, P.B., Fischer, U., Habich, D., Lehner, W.: Efficient in-memory indexing with generalized prefix trees. In: Härder, T., Lehner, W., Mitschang, B., Schöning, H., Schwarz, H. (eds.) BTW. LNI, vol. 180, pp. 227–246. GI, Kaiserslautern (2011)
2. Färber, F., Cha, S.K., Primsch, J., Bornhövd, C., Sigg, S., Lehner, W.: SAP HANA database: data management for modern business applications. SIGMOD Rec. **40**(4), 45–51 (2011)
3. Faust, M., Schwalb, D., Krueger, J., Plattner, H.: Fast lookups for in-memory column stores: group-key indices, lookup and maintenance. In: ADMS 2012
4. Grund, M., Krueger, J., Plattner, H., Zeier, A., Cudre-Mauroux, P., Madden, S.: HYRISE—a main memory hybrid storage engine. In: VLDB 2010 (2010)
5. Krüger, J., Kim, C., Grund, M., Satish, N., Schwalb, D., Chhugani, J., Plattner, H., Dubey, P., Zeier, A.: Fast updates on read-optimized databases using multi-core CPUs. PVLDB **5**(1), 61–72 (2011)
6. Leis, V., Kemper, A., Neumann, T.: The adaptive radix tree: artful indexing for main-memory databases. In: Jensen, C.S., Jermaine, C.M., Zhou, X. (eds.) ICDE, pp. 38–49. IEEE Computer Society (2013)
7. Müller, I., Ratsch, C., Faerber, F.: Adaptive string dictionary compression in in-memory column-store database systems. In: EDBT (2014)
8. Raman, V., Attaluri, G., Barber, R., Chainani, N., Kalmuk, D., KulandaiSamy, V., Leenstra, J., Lightstone, S., Liu, S., Lohman, G.M., Malkemus, T., Mueller, R., Pandis, I., Schiefer, B., Sharpe, D., Sidle, R., Storm, A., Zhang, L.: DB2 with BLU acceleration: so much more than just a column store. In: Proceedings of the VLDB Endowment, pp. 1080–1091. VLDB Endowment, Aug 2013
9. Raman, V., Swart, G., Qiao, L., Reiss, F., Dialani, V., Kossmann, D., Narang, I., Sidle, R.: Constant-time query processing. In: ICDE 2008: Proceedings of the 2008 IEEE 24th International Conference on Data Engineering. IEEE Computer Society, Apr 2008
10. Rao, J., Ross, K.: Cache conscious indexing for decision-support in main memory. In: Proceedings of the International Conference on Very Large Data Bases (VLDB) (1999)
11. Rao, J., Ross, K.A.: Making B+-Trees Cache Conscious in Main Memory, vol. 29. ACM, New York (2000)
12. Sikka, V., Färber, F., Lehner, W., Cha, S.K., Peh, T., Bornhövd, C.: Efficient transaction processing in SAP HANA database: the end of a column store myth. In: Candan, K.S., Chen, Y., Snodgrass, R.T., Gravano, L., Fuxman, A. (eds.) SIGMOD Conference, pp. 731–742. ACM, New York (2012)

Author Index

Printed in the United States
By Bookmasters